Photograph by Denis De Marney

ACT I (*from left to right*) COLIN GORDON, EUGENE DECKERS, THEODORE BIKEL AND ALAN GIFFORD.

THE LOVE OF FOUR COLONELS

A Play in Three Acts

by

PETER USTINOV

For Richard E. Myers
of New York

ENGLISH THEATRE GUILD LTD.
ASCOT HOUSE, 52 DEAN STREET, LONDON, W.1

*For information regarding the acting fee payable on each and
every performance of this play, and any other particulars, application
must be made to the publishers :—*

ENGLISH THEATRE GUILD LTD.
Ascot House, 52 Dean Street, London, W.1.

**No performance can be given unless a licence is first of all
obtained.**

Fees are payable in advance.

**Licences will be issued on receipt of remittance provided the
following details are forwarded :**

> *Date or dates of performance.*
> *Name of theatre or hall or full address.*
> *Name of Society.*

Copyright, Peter Ustinov, 1951.

Printed in Great Britain by the Whitefriars Press Ltd.
London and Tonbridge

This play was presented by Linnit and Dunfee Ltd. (by arrangement with Bronson Albery) at Wyndham's Theatre on May 23rd, 1951, with the following cast :—

COLONEL DESMOND DE S. RINDER-SPARROW	*Colin Gordon*
COLONEL WESLEY BREITENSPIEGEL	*Alan Gifford*
COLONEL AIMÉ FRAPPOT	*Eugene Deckers*
COLONEL ALEXANDER IKONENKO	*Theodore Bikel*
THE MAYOR OF HERZOGENBURG	*Paul Hardtmuth*
THE WICKED FAIRY	*Peter Ustinov*
THE GOOD FAIRY	*Gwen Cherrell*
THE BEAUTY	*Moira Lister*
MRS. BREITENSPIEGEL	*Patricia Jessel*
MME. FRAPPOT	*Diana Graves*
MRS. RINDER-SPARROW	*Mary Hignett*
MME. IKONENKO	*Mona Lilian*

The play produced by *John Fernald*

Settings designed by *Fanny Taylor*

Music specially composed by *Antony Hopkins*

SYNOPSIS OF SCENES

ACT I: *The Office of the Allied Administration at Herzogenberg.*

ACT II: *Within the Castle.*

ACT III: *The same. A few minutes later.*

THE LOVE OF FOUR COLONELS

ACT I.

The offices of the Allied Military Administration at Herzogenburg, a village in the Hartz mountains, disputed by Britain, France, America and Russia after the Great War of 1939–45. As a consequence of this dispute on a high level, this innocent and charming spot is cursed with an abundance of Colonels, charged by their governments to carry on the friction on an intimate, domestic level. The scene of the battleground is a drab room giving every evidence of near-destruction, but rendered habitable by a liberal dispensation of plywood, cardboard, and asbestos. The furnishing is as functional as only military interior decoration can be. There is a trestle-table, four chairs, a few ingenious filing-systems in cupboardlike containers. The walls are covered in old notices, all of them either urgent or important. There is also a large photograph of a naked woman being coy with a beach ball, a drawing of a bulldog with young, a reproduction of an Utrillo street-scene, and a framed portrait of Joseph Stalin. The window at the back gives over a forest. The upper turrets of a castle can be dimly perceived rising from the jungle.

Door L. *Door* R.

As the curtain rises, COLONEL WESLEY BREITENSPIEGEL *is lying back dangerously in his chair, his feet on the table, smoking a cigar. He is a bald man with rimless glasses.* COLONEL DESMOND DE S. RINDER-SPARROW *is sitting forward on the very edge of his chair, puffing at a pipe, his eyes glazed in the manner of an Empirebuilder hypnotized by his greatest enemy, the horizon. There follows the longest pause in theatrical history, towards the end of which the audience should be convinced that the actors have been the victims of some administrative disaster. The pause is terminated after the adequate time for embarrassment has elapsed.*

DESMOND.   We seem to have run out of conversation.

(*Another long pause.*)

WESLEY.   Yeah . . .
DESMOND.   What ?
WESLEY.   Yeah . . .
DESMOND.   Yes . . .

(*Pause.*)

WESLEY.   Have you ever contemplated suicide ?
DESMOND (*deeply interested*).   Lord no.   Have you ?
WESLEY.   No.
DESMOND.   I say, old man, you're not . . . I mean . . .
WESLEY (*a little irritated*).   What are you so embarrassed about ?
DESMOND.   Well, I hardly like to say.
WESLEY.   Then don't.
DESMOND.   You've not anything rash in mind ?
WESLEY.   No.   Unless you call playing golf with you rash.
DESMOND.   That's very far from what I meant.   This sudden mention of suicide . . .
WESLEY.   Oh, no.   Good God, no.   My wife would be furious.

(DESMOND *laughs.*)

What are you laughing at ?
DESMOND.   You bringing the wife into it.
WESLEY.   My wife's not funny.   She's very far from funny. But then I don't go for laughter much.   I'm a romantic at heart.

(DESMOND *laughs again.*)

What are you snickering at now ?
DESMOND.   I always imagined a romantic as tall and emaciated, with long hair.
WESLEY.   Do you mean to say you haven't even gotten the imagination to conceive of a bald romantic ?
DESMOND.   I've never given the matter a thought, to tell you the honest truth.
WESLEY (*robust*).   Then it's time you did !   You have before

you a man who dreams of only one thing—to disobey an order in the most glamorous possible way.

DESMOND (*shocked*). Disobey an order ?

WESLEY. Yes . . . I'd like to have led the Charge of the Light Brigade against all expert advice.

DESMOND (*possessive*). You'd have to have been a British officer to do that.

WESLEY. You're as possessive as a woman.

DESMOND. I'm quoting facts.

WESLEY. O.K., O.K. I'll leave the Charge of the Light Brigade to you.

DESMOND. I don't particularly want it.

WESLEY. And you grudge me having it ?

DESMOND. Oh, you can have it if you like.

WESLEY. Now I'm sore. I don't want it any more.

DESMOND. I'm sorry. I didn't mean to be difficult about it.

WESLEY (*defiant*). I still have Custer's Last Stand.

DESMOND. Yes, I suppose you have.

WESLEY. Listen, I'll tell you just how romantic I am.

DESMOND. Are you positive you haven't told me before ?

WESLEY. You know, you're the one man who's ever made me lose my taste for conversation.

DESMOND. I've always preferred silence myself.

WESLEY (*vindictive*). In that case, I'm sorry to disappoint you.

DESMOND. I'm used to disappointment, old fellow.

WESLEY. Well, I'm not. My romanticism is entirely personal and selfish. It is, according to my psychiatrist, ingrowing, largely owing to the inadequacy of my father.

DESMOND. He seems to have been adequate enough to bring you into the world.

WESLEY. He was counter-balanced by the overadequacy of my mother, and of a certain Doctor Purkiss.

DESMOND. Was he the family doctor ?

WESLEY. In more ways than one.

DESMOND. Good gracious me.

WESLEY. A compromise was reached. My second name is Purkiss.

DESMOND. How very unusual.

WESLEY. My psychiatrist assures me it is absolutely usual, and that it is wrong to conceal such things, as a lack of ventilation alone breeds complexes. Have you a psychiatrist ?

DESMOND. In England we can't afford them. Thank God.

(COLONEL AIMÉ FRAPPOT *enters. Short and a little sour, a dead cigarette always in his mouth.*)

Hello, Aimé.

AIMÉ.   Ikonenko not here yet ?

DESMOND.   No sign of him.

AIMÉ.   The conference should have begun five minutes ago. I hoped I would be late.

DESMOND (*smiling*).   Not looking forward to it ?

AIMÉ.   Enormously.   Last week we all talked in French.   For once I could relax and tell you all what I thought of you with no fear of contradiction.

DESMOND.   It beats me why we should have to talk French when all of you know English.

AIMÉ.   It is a question of honour.   English may be more convenient, but it will not be used if there is the chance of the French language being slighted.

(*He feels in his pocket for a match, and not finding one, goes over to* DESMOND, *who is lighting his pipe.*)

May I ?

(DESMOND *gives him a light.*)

WESLEY.   Next week we all have to speak Russian.

AIMÉ.   It's then that Ikonenko pushes all his legislation through, and we get into trouble.

WESLEY.   Yeah.   The bastard.

AIMÉ.   He's not a bad fellow.

DESMOND.   Clever.

AIMÉ.   We mustn't be ungenerous enough to grudge him that.

WESLEY.   After all, we're all clever in our own way.

AIMÉ (*with a smile and a glance at* WESLEY).   Yes.   (*Slight pause.*)   It's strange how I hate this place, and yet I know in advance I'll be sorry to leave it.

DESMOND.   Yes, it is strange.

AIMÉ.   No, not really.   It was stupid of me to say it was strange.   Have you never noticed how, in life, hatred is as binding a tie as love ?   The pathos of leaving a detested school, or a mistress who has begun to bore you ?

DESMOND (*charming*).   Heavens, I always begin to bore them first.

AIMÉ (*a little disarmed*). I must remember that. It's a perfectly charming remark.

DESMOND (*surprised*). Is it?

WESLEY. Why did you go into the Army, Aimé?

AIMÉ. My father said it was the best entrée into politics. He was a man hypnotized by his own mediocrity.

DESMOND. Oh, I say. Those are hard words for anyone to use about his old man. What was he?

AIMÉ. He was Minister of Agriculture for ten minutes in 1912.

(*The others laugh.*)

You know, Desmond, you look like a man who has never had the embarrassment of a choice in his life.

DESMOND. Well, in my case it was a toss-up between the Army and the Church. Luckily there were more vacancies in the Army at that particular moment, so my mind was made up for me. I wasn't very bright, you understand.

AIMÉ (*with tact*). I understand entirely.

DESMOND (*suddenly laughing*). Before you came in, Wesley said he was a romantic.

AIMÉ. I know he is.

DESMOND (*unsure now*). Is he?

AIMÉ. Yes. He's a romantic. I'm a realist. And you . . . you're a thoroughly nice fellow.

DESMOND (*barely audible*). Thanks.

AIMÉ. That's why we get on so badly. Think of us, for a moment, and reflect on the stupidity of our employers. We have been here ever since this disputed zone was created, two and a half years ago, and in that time we have decided nothing except that we wish to transfer our headquarters from here to that overgrown palace. (*He gazes at it through the window.*)

WESLEY. I've had the latest reports in from the troops trying to get through to the castle.

AIMÉ. Any result?

WESLEY. No. Lieutenant Coppermaker reports that at first he thought the weeds uprooted during the day were being replaced in some mysterious way by the local population during the night. Now he's convinced the plants are growing together by themselves during the hours of darkness. He then indulges in some useless speculation on the effect of the atomic explosion on flora and fauna, and suggests finally that Washington should send a man.

DESMOND. Is it going to ?

WESLEY. If you knew Washington, you'd realize that that is the silliest thing to ask it to do. What I've done is to send Lieutenant Coppermaker to the psychiatrist for a start.

AIMÉ (*smiles*). You are sceptical because you are a romantic. I, being a realist, am prepared to accept Lieutenant Coppermaker's report.

WESLEY. What do you mean ?

AIMÉ (*agreeable*). I believe in fairies.

DESMOND. Well, you know, in Ireland——

WESLEY. I know, leprechauns, giants. Listen to me——

(*The door opens, and* COLONEL IKONENKO *enters. An entirely expressionless man carrying a brief case. There is an electric silence occasioned by his entrance.*)

You're late.

(IKONENKO *doesn't answer. He just sits at his place, spreads his papers out, opens his fountain pen, and then says :*)

IKONENKO. Now you're late.

(*The others all make haste to sit down.*)

Colonel Breitenspiegel, I wish to bring to your attention as Chairman for this week that I am Chairman by rotation next week, and that the official language for the seven days commencing (*He consults a diary*) on the 18th will be Russian.

WESLEY. There's no need to rub that in.

AIMÉ. Colonel Ikonenko, may I permit myself the honour of bringing to your kind attention the fact that during the week commencing (*He consults a diary*) the 2nd, that is, eight days after the conclusion of your term as Chairman, I shall be in the Chair, and the recognized language will be French.

IKONENKO (*stiff*). That is generally understood.

DESMOND. I trust no-one is forgetting that (*flicking the pages of his diary*). Where are we ?—Yes—that on the 25th it's my turn, and we all speak English.

AIMÉ. On behalf of my Government, I agree.

WESLEY. There's no need to put all this to the vote, I trust.

IKONENKO (*secretive*). It may be better.

WESLEY. But heavens, we all agree.

IKONENKO. You never know.

WESLEY. Well, I'm against it. It's ridiculous. It's a waste of time.

IKONENKO. I must insist.

WESLEY. In that case, I propose that this Committee does not wish to vote on the agreement of the agreement, owing to the redundancy of so doing. Will all in favour of not voting kindly signify their viewpoint in the usual way ?

(WESLEY, DESMOND *and* AIMÉ *raise their hands.*)

Now will all in favour of voting raise their hands ?

(IKONENKO *lifts his hand.*)

The Committee has voted by a majority of three to one not to vote.

(IKONENKO *packs all his documents, and leaves the room.*)

Crazy guy.

AIMÉ. He'll be back in a minute.

DESMOND. Extraordinary waste of energy.

(*Pause.* IKONENKO *re-enters, and replaces all his documents expressionlessly.*)

IKONENKO. What is next on the agenda ?

WESLEY. You haven't given me much time to look up my notes, have you ?

IKONENKO. Is there any report on the state of the castle yet from your subordinate ?

WESLEY. Yes. All in good time.

IKONENKO. I must take it on myself to press for a decision.

WESLEY. Another matter comes first on the agenda.

IKONENKO. I must press for a reversal in the order of the agenda.

WESLEY (*angry*). Why ?

IKONENKO. I have received a report on the situation independently of yours. Lieutenant of the 3rd Grade Bulganov——

WESLEY (*livid*). That is a direct contravention of our agreement that the duty of investigating and clearing the undergrowth surrounding the castle devolved on United States arms. Lieutenant Coppermaker was acting not in the interests of the U.S., but in the interests of the——

IKONENKO (*firm*).   Lieutenant of the 3rd Grade Bulganov's word is above suspicion.   He is a Hero of Stalingrad, a Hero of Labour, and holder of the Suvorov Medal of the 2nd Class.

WESLEY.   That has nothing to do with it !   Lieutenant Coppermaker is an accredited member of the New York Stock Exchange, and an old Princeton alumnus.   His report is the only valid report, and the matter will be dealt with in the order of the agenda.

AIMÉ.   I thought you said he had been sent to the psychiatrist ?

WESLEY (*faltering*).   On a social call.   The psychiatrist is an old personal friend of his.

AIMÉ.   From the Stock Exchange ?

WESLEY.   No, from Princeton.

IKONENKO.   You refuse to change the order of the agenda ?

WESLEY.   As Chairman for the week, I formally refuse your request.

(IKONENKO *gathers all his papers together, and leaves the room.*)

Will you get him !

DESMOND.   It's damn bad form, you know.

AIMÉ.   He believes in exercise.

(IKONENKO *returns, expressionless, and lays his documents on the table.*)

IKONENKO.   What is the next subject for discussion ?

WESLEY.   I'm going to give way to you, Ikonenko.   We're going to discuss the castle after all.   I'm sick and tired of you, and I'm going to have this out with you, here and now.   I will begin with Lieutenant Coppermaker's report.   Mummummummum . . . (*He skips passages which seem to him irrelevant.*). . . " In that I am convinced after three days' work on the undergrowth, during which we employed not only picks and shovels, but also bulldozers and tractors, that some botanical phenomenon is restricting our progress.   However many weeds we dug up during the day, they were without exception deep in the soil again next morning.   It is clear to anyone with an elementary knowledge of gardening that the reconstitution of the weeds is far neater and more accurate than could be achieved by human labour. I therefore feel . . . " mummummummum . . . that is Lieutenant Coppermaker's report in a nutshell.

IKONENKO.   Colonel Breitenspiegel, we are here to put our cards on the table. There is no room in our relationship for nutshells. Why, Colonel Breitenspiegel, were you mumbling?

WESLEY.   Red tape, Colonel Ikonenko. Unadulterated military red tape, with which, for reasons of a surprising charity, I did not wish to try your patience!

IKONENKO.   Your attitude is deeply unpleasant to me. Rather than argue with you, I will set you an example. Contrary to the hysteria shown by Lieutenant Coppermaker, the report of Lieutenant of the 3rd Grade Bulganov is both brilliant and to the point. (*He opens a document.*) Mummummummum . . . " It is easy to understand that the lack of progress in the clearing of the undergrowth is due to—(1) the lack of will to work shown by American soldiers unversed in Socialist doctrine, (2) the consistent sabotage exercised by Reactionary Diversionists and Fascist hyenas . . . "

(WESLEY *opens his mouth to reply, but is too late.*)

DESMOND.   Nobody with a working knowledge of the hyena would ever credit it with any political opinions.

WESLEY (*angry*).   Desmond, for God's sake don't interrupt. What was the meaning of all *that* mumbling, Ikonenko? Here's something I want to put to the vote, fellows.

IKONENKO.   I object.

WESLEY.   I move that this meeting deplores the underhand, surreptitious and dishonest nature of the Soviet tactics on the occasion of the report over the operations to free the castle from its surrounding jungle. Will all those in favour kindly raise their hands?

(WESLEY *and* DESMOND *raise their hands, but* AIMÉ *rises and goes towards the door. There is immediate tension. All half-rise.*)

IKONENKO.   Does this move of yours reflect the official French attitude?

AIMÉ.   What?

WESLEY.   Does this mean a split in the Atlantic bloc?

AIMÉ.   Why?

IKONENKO. I must telegraph Moscow immediately.

AIMÉ. For what reason ?

WESLEY. I warn you, this action may affect United States Economic Aid.

AIMÉ. What action ?

DESMOND. Remember Verdun, old son. Don't let us down now !

AIMÉ. Who am I letting down ?

WESLEY. Us. By walking out of the conference now, of all times.

AIMÉ. There comes a time during the day when even the most strongly constituted of us has to leave the room. I'll be back in a minute.

(AIMÉ *goes out*.)

WESLEY. There are times when nature reasserts herself, Ikonenko, and laughs in the face of all governments. That should be a chastening thought for you.

IKONENKO. The Soviet Government has never attempted to deny the presence of nature in the world. On the other hand, we are the pioneers of Socialist-Realism, and the dishonest manner in which Colonel Frappot left the room reflects the mocking and decadent state of contemporary French so-called civilization.

DESMOND. How does a Socialist-Realist spend a penny ?

IKONENKO. I do not understand the question.

WESLEY. What would you have done ?

IKONENKO. I should have made my intention clear.

DESMOND. How terribly embarrassing.

WESLEY. Speaking then as a Socialist-Realist——

IKONENKO. But you are not one.

WESLEY. O.K. Speaking as a—what is it ? Pluto-Democrat——

IKONENKO. You condemn yourself !

WESLEY. It's rather fun. I like it. Speaking as one of those, I think Stalin stinks.

IKONENKO. I think the same of Truman.

WESLEY. So do I. I'm a Republican.

(AIMÉ *returns*.)

AIMÉ. The Mayor is waiting outside . . . did any one of you summon him ?

WESLEY. I did, yes.

IKONENKO. Without consulting us ?

WESLEY. Have him come in. (*To* IKONENKO.) If you walk out now, you'll miss the fun.

(AIMÉ *goes to the door, and returns with the* MAYOR OF HERZO-GENBURG. *Very old, very benevolent.*)

Dr. Busch, why come right in.

MAYOR (*beaming*). So nice. (*He shakes* WESLEY *by the hand.*) Oberst Breitenspiegel. Your name I remember. It's a good old German name.

WESLEY. We're descended from the Counts of Breitenspiegel.

MAYOR. This I didn't know. But once we had, when I was small, a man who was sharpening the knives in the village. He had exactly this name of Breitenspiegel.

WESLEY. Yes . . . well, you know Colonel Frappot.

MAYOR. Oh, yes. (*In appalling French.*) Chay eu l'honneur de vous regontrer . . . em . . . decha . . .

AIMÉ. En effet, M. le Maire.

DESMOND. Good evening, Mr. Mayor.

WESLEY. Colonel Rinder-Sparrow.

MAYOR (*laughing*). You must forgive it to me. Such a name I can't not so remember. Breitenspiegel— —

WESLEY. Colonel Ikonenko.

(IKONENKO *doesn't look up.*)

MAYOR (*determined to make an impression*). Da, da, da. Nitchevo. Ya Vas Lublu.

WESLEY. Won't you sit down ?

IKONENKO. I must make my position clear. I am opposed to your visit here.

MAYOR. Why ?

IKONENKO. I was not consulted.

MAYOR (*pityingly*). Is that the only reason ?

WESLEY. Others will occur to him later on. Come on, sit down. Have a cigar. Now, Herr Busch, we'll come straight to the point.

MAYOR (*with the infinite indulgence of the older man*). You wish to ask questions from the castle, naturally.

DESMOND. How do you know ?

IKONENKO. Nothing is confidential in this place.

MAYOR.   Oh, my dear boy, why should it be ? I have been an officer in an army of occupation myself—Galicia, 1914.   No, dear boys, if you have secrets, you keep them from each other, not from me.

(THE COLONELS *shift nervously*.)

WESLEY.   Suppose you tell us about the castle ?

MAYOR.   Forget the castle.   I have seen your soldiers working, and I even saw a Russian officer sitting in the bushes looking at them, and I thought to myself, " So much sweat wasted, and that poor officer can sit in the bush all night, he will find nothing. Nothing."

WESLEY.   Why nothing ?

MAYOR.   Don't ask me.   Even if I knew——

IKONENKO.   He's bluffing.

MAYOR (*strange*).   I know nothing about it.

WESLEY.   But you do know that the weeds around it behave in the strangest way.

IKONENKO (*loud*).   He knows ?   He is responsible for it !

MAYOR.   I know it is difficult to reach the castle . . .

WESLEY.   Difficult ?   It's damned impossible !

MAYOR.   I have never tried it myself.

WESLEY.   Why not ?   I should have thought that human inquisitiveness alone would have——

MAYOR.   In these parts we know better than to try.   We leave it to the others.

AIMÉ (*intrigued*).   Which others ?

MAYOR.   The officials.   People like you.   There was a Gauleiter who came here eight years ago.   He saw it in the distance and wanted it as his office.   He tried to enter, and failed.

DESMOND.   Good heavens, we're not in Tibet.   What is all this mystery ?

MAYOR.   Before him, there was an officer of the Gestapo who came here.   Once again he tried, and once again he failed.   He is now in a lunatic asylum.

WESLEY.   Why ?

MAYOR.   It was the shock of failure on a mentality at that time accustomed to success.

IKONENKO.   Herr Busch, you have spoken to us in a deeply suspicious and incomprehensible manner, and your attitude, even though it is impossible to understand, does you no credit   I must warn you against the terrible danger of being incomprehensible in the future.

MAYOR. I am not afraid of you, dear child. Why do you want to take what does not belong to you ?

WESLEY. That's no way to talk, Mayor. You must understand that Germany has been thrashed, and that we're here as an occupying force. You've got no right to argue with us.

MAYOR. You have defeated Germany, but you have not defeated me, and you have not defeated the past, and you have not defeated the soil.

DESMOND. Now look here, Mr. Mayor, you inferred, if I understood you aright, that we are thieves. As I understand it, that castle doesn't belong to anyone—who then are we robbing ?

MAYOR. You are robbing history.

DESMOND. That's nonsense.

AIMÉ. But it's extremely poetic.

IKONENKO. Poetry should be left to poets.

AIMÉ. Why ?

IKONENKO. It is their duty. Our duty is administration. Regardless of any decision of this Council, I shall give the order to-night for Soviet troops at my disposal to begin operations for the occupation of the castle at dawn to-morrow, so that it may pass back into the hands of its legitimate owners, the people !

(*The* MAYOR *laughs.*)

Your laughter may have serious consequences.

MAYOR. You say the castle belongs to the people. How will they all get into it ?

AIMÉ (*who has been pacing agitatedly*). I ask you, mon Colonel, to reconsider your order to your troops.

IKONENKO. Actions are more comprehensible than words !

AIMÉ. And more dangerous.

IKONENKO. The victors must educate the defeated. Our position here has been made ridiculous by (1) the lack of initiative shown by American troops in clearing the undergrowth, and (2) the Wall Street tactics of——

WESLEY (*jumping up*). I've had enough of this !

DESMOND (*jumping up*). May I appeal for some good sound British common sense ?

IKONENKO. What have you to say ?

DESMOND. Nothing as yet, but I'm thinking furiously.

(WESLEY *draws some pills out of his pocket, and an inhaler. Quickly
he takes the pills.*)

MAYOR (*soft*).   Dear boys, you are making yourselves ill, and
all for such silly reasons. You must take care of yourselves. Are
you married ?   Colonel Ikonenko ?

IKONENKO.   I do not discuss my affairs in public.

MAYOR.   Your wife is an official secret also ?

(WESLEY *inhales deeply, shutting first one nostril, then the other.*)

AIMÉ.   I am married.   We are all married.

MAYOR.   And you are happy ?

AIMÉ.   Speaking personally, she is the mother of my children.

MAYOR.   And that is all ?

AIMÉ.   I live with an actress. She lives with a haulage-
contractor. Apart from that we are inseparable.

MAYOR.   But your children ?

AIMÉ (*simply*).   I love them.

DESMOND.   What has all this to do with the castle ?

MAYOR.   A great deal, Colonel. Have you a wife and a home ?

DESMOND.   Yes, and three dogs.

MAYOR.   And you love them ?

DESMOND.   Yes, I breed them. Dingos. Wild dogs, you know.

MAYOR.   And I presume that Herr Breitenspiegel is also
married ?

WESLEY.   Don't talk to me. The doctor told me I've got to be
free from all worry.

MAYOR.   Then as you all have something worth living for,
children, I beg you not to continue asking questions about the
castle. Be happy you are alive, and leave it at that. I appeal to
you before it's too late !

DESMOND.   Too late ? Too late for what ?

MAYOR (*very soft*). . . . All I know is that when I was telling
the Gauleiter what I had heard about the castle, the door opened
slowly without us noticing it . . .

(*The door begins to open slowly.*)

AIMÉ.   And who came in ?

MAYOR (*his voice filled with wonder*).   Nobody . . .

(IKONENKO *suddenly laughs.*)

IKONENKO. Brilliantly dramatic !
DESMOND. Who opened that door ?
IKONENKO. The wind.
AIMÉ (*at the window*). Look at the trees. There's no wind
to-day.
MAYOR (*agonized*). Oh my dear children, change the subject !
AIMÉ. What happened then ?
MAYOR. A bell rang. A terrible, cracked church bell.
IKONENKO (*after a pause. Triumphant.*) Silence !

(*A distant church bell rings a discordant note.*)

MAYOR (*vehement*). You fools !
AIMÉ (*shouting*). What happened then ?

(*The figure of a* MAN *appears silently at the door, dressed as a tramp.
He is very tall, thin, and he smiles. The* MAYOR *expresses the
greatest terror, cowers, crosses himself, places his hat on his head,
and prepares to escape.*)

MAN (*calm*). Guten abend, Herr Busch.

(THE MAYOR *lifts his hat.*)

MAYOR. Guten abend . . .

(*He runs out.*)

IKONENKO. Who are you ? And have you a permit ?
MAN. I have many permits to do many things, but I can afford
to ignore them.
IKONENKO. No, my friend, you cannot afford to ignore them.
You may not circulate without a permit, and you may not enter
this office without an appointment.
MAN. I have an appointment.
IKONENKO. We never make appointments during conference
hours.
MAN. All you need do is to look in your appointment book.
IKONENKO. No use, I know we have no appointments. Now
will you kindly leave before I call soldiers.

MAN. Your soldiers are all asleep. I passed them on the way up, sleeping like babies.

IKONENKO. What? You're lying!

MAN. Oh, you nasty man. What a horrid thing to say!

DESMOND (*who has been fingering the appointment book*). I say, it's quite true.

IKONENKO. What?

DESMOND. There is an appointment here.

WESLEY. For whom?

DESMOND. I don't know. It's in Russian.

IKONENKO. Let me see.

(DESMOND *passes the book.*)

Professor Diabolikov. I did not write this.

DESMOND. It's in your handwriting, old son.

IKONENKO. Diabolikov. Is that your name?

MAN. It was a nickname Catherine the Great gave me . . . to please Voltaire. They shared the joke. I never thought it very funny.

IKONENKO. I must warn you——

MAN. Against the dangers of incomprehensibility. I know.

IKONENKO. What? (*Fresh start.*) Are you a Russian subject?

MAN. Not predominantly.

IKONENKO. I expect a specific answer.

MAN. I expect an intelligent question, duckie.

DESMOND. I regret to say the fellow's English.

MAN. Not unqualifiedly, I'm just talking English because this is the week for talking English. If you had inspired a visit next week, I should have talked Russian with pleasure.

AIMÉ. How did you know about our ruling?

MAN. How did I know . . . and love . . . Catherine the Great?

AIMÉ. Love?

MAN. In my way . . .

AIMÉ. Vous l'avez aimé?

MAN (*in perfect French*). À ma façon . . .

IKONENKO. You have not yet produced a satisfactory permit.

MAN (*searching in his vast coat*). You really are most difficult to convince. What's this?

(*He pulls out a scroll.*)

Oh, no. This is permission from Nero to taunt the lions before their dinner of gospellers. Here we are. No. A front-row ticket for Robespierre's execution. A disappointing affair. The weather was far from perfect. There's a special kind of weather which is ideal for executions, you know—you need an autumn morning, really, to surround the scene with an aura of poetic melancholy, and just enough of an orange sun to catch the blade. For lions, on the other hand, you can't do better than your mid-summer heat, in which the poor beasts are torn between an oppressive lethargy and their greed for blood. Such leonine quandaries drag out the agony of the gospellers deliciously. (*With a giggle.*) But what am I doing, talking about it as though it still went on to-day. No, alas. (*He sighs.*) The taste for limited horror was dissipated. A decadence set in. Our love of quality was polluted by a love of quantity. Nowadays we do things on a majestic scale, with guns and bombs and gasses, and it's surprising how the human species obeys our every whim in this respect . . . (*Looking at the* COLONELS.) All dressed up in their little boiler suits, with bits of gold and silver braid to mark the degree of their guilt. (*He laughs.*) Oh dear, oh dear . . .

IKONENKO (*terrible*). Where is the permit ?

MAN (*feminine*). Oh, do stop nagging, Sasha ! I've got it. Look. Signed by you. (*He gives* IKONENKO *a permit.*) This man may go anywhere, do anything and say anything at any time. Signed Ikonenko.

IKONENKO (*his hand trembling*). This permit is a forgery, and is confiscated.

MAN. I don't mind. I've got plenty more. Look, here's the same signed by Stalin, on official paper.

(IKONENKO *seizes it.*)

IKONENKO. This permit is likewise——

MAN (*sinister*). Be careful what you say ! Do you dare to suggest that this is a forgery too ? (*In terribly accurate and menacing Russian.*) Astarojna, Tovarisch Polkovnik ! (*He wags a finger.*) Astarojna ! I may well be an officer of the M.V.D. You never can be sure.

IKONENKO. The situation is open to review.

WESLEY. What does that mean ?

IKONENKO. This is a purely Soviet matter.

DESMOND. I damn well *hope* it is.

IKONENKO. The conditions in this town are perilous for visitors. I therefore take the liberty of placing you in protective custody until it is safe for you to circulate.

(*He rings a bell.*)

MAN. I told you the soldiers were asleep. Nobody will answer that bell.

IKONENKO. We shall see.

MAN (*offering* DESMOND *a pouch*). Tobacco, Colonel?

DESMOND. Thank you so much. I only smoke my own brand.

MAN. McPherson's Fine Old Curly Shag.

DESMOND. How did you know?

MAN. It's the only kind I have.

DESMOND. But it's unobtainable outside the Shetland Islands.

MAN. I know. Isn't it a bore. (*He gives* DESMOND *the pouch. To* WESLEY.) Cigar?

WESLEY (*challenging*). I bet you don't have my brand.

MAN. Cherokee Blues?

WESLEY. Well, what do you know?

(*The* MAN *throws it over.*)

MAN. Mon Colonel, Gauloise Bleue?

AIMÉ (*pleasant*). Je ne dirai pas non.

MAN (*giving him the packet of cigarettes*). Voilà. Comrade Colonel.

IKONENKO. I don't smoke.

MAN. I have even catered for you. I have brought you nothing.

(IKONENKO *rings the bell again, viciously.*)

DESMOND. I say, I've been thinking.

MAN. Yes?

DESMOND. It's just occurred to me . . .

MAN. Yes?

DESMOND. Who are you?

MAN (*sighing sadly*). It's a long story.

AIMÉ. How long?

MAN (*a little surprised*). Very, very long.

AIMÉ. I have no light.

MAN. Oh, I'm so sorry.

(*He pulls out an enormous and elaborate table lighter from his robes which gives a flame like a blow-lamp. They all gaze at it in astonishment. With some trepidation* AIMÉ *lights his cigarette from it. Pause.*)

AIMÉ. Do you know who I think you are ?
MAN. No.
AIMÉ. The devil.

(*The* MAN *practically drops the lighter.*)

MAN (*falsetto*). Who ?
AIMÉ (*charming*). The devil.
MAN. Why, do I look like him ?
DESMOND. I say, steady.
AIMÉ. I don't know. I've never met him. But he's someone I've always wanted to meet. We have so much in common.
MAN. I'm glad you've never met him, dear, because I've never heard that I look like him before, even from those who know us both very well. I don't want to seem catty, or say anything behind his back which could give offence, because I have the very, very highest regard for him, but I don't think looks are his strong point. Dear me, no.
DESMOND. This is perfectly preposterous. I suppose the next thing you'll be telling us is that you know God.
MAN (*sore point*). I always go out of my way to smile at Him, but He *always* cuts me dead.
IKONENKO (*who has been ringing furiously*). This man is mad. I am going to fetch the soldiers.
MAN. Sorry if I've been boring you about God and the Devil— I beg your pardon, the Devil and God.
IKONENKO. I recognize no such people.

(*He stamps out.*)

AIMÉ. But then, who are you ?
WESLEY. He's come straight out of an asylum.
DESMOND. How d'you explain all those tricks of his ? How d'you explain the tobacco ?

WESLEY. He's a conjuror who's gone crazy. Yeah, that's it, the guy's a crazy conjuror.

DESMOND. It goes deeper than that, I'm afraid, Wesley. This tobacco. It's the genuine article. Marvellous. It takes a lot to convince me, but now . . .

AIMÉ. What has he convinced you of ?

DESMOND. I don't know yet . . .

(*They look at the* MAN *fixedly. He becomes coy.*)

MAN. You're making my ears tingle, talking about me like that.

WESLEY. Why did you come here ?

MAN. In answer to a summons.

WESLEY. Who summoned you ?

MAN. I came to take you to the castle.

DESMOND. The castle !

(IKONENKO *returns.*)

IKONENKO. All the soldiers have been drugged ! This is sabotage and counter-revolutionary activity of the most dangerous sort. (*To the* MAN.) You are under arrest.

MAN. Don't be silly.

(*The* MAN *rises.*)

IKONENKO. Stay where you are !

MAN. I want to stretch my legs.

IKONENKO (*draws a revolver. He shouts*). Stay where you are !

DESMOND.⎫ Ikonenko !

WESLEY.   ⎬ Put that away !

AIMÉ.   ⎭ I forbid it !

MAN. Don't worry about me. (*Approaches* IKONENKO.) Now, don't make a fool of yourself, there's a love.

(IKONENKO *shoots once ; twice ; then four times in rapid succession.
The* MAN *scratches his stomach.*)

(*Feline*). It's terrible how bullets tickle.

IKONENKO (*appalled*). He's alive ! (*He collapses on to a sofa.*)

DESMOND (*military*). Explain yourself.

MAN. Who ?

DESMOND. You, sir.

MAN. Me ?

DESMOND. Yes, indeed, sir. Why aren't you dead ?

MAN. Why should I be ?

DESMOND. Don't side-step the issue, sir. This is the most inconsiderate behaviour. After all, we are in some sense allied to the Russians, and look what you've done to my friend over there.

(IKONENKO *is in a state of collapse.*)

He's in a perfectly ghastly condition. What you've done, sir, is neither fair nor funny. I can only put it down to a lack of breeding. Now, out with it !

MAN. Out with what ? I have it on the devil's authority that English women are the easiest of victims, while Englishmen are quite impossibly difficult in practically every respect.

DESMOND. I will not tolerate remarks of a questionable nature about my countrywomen from the devil or anyone else. Kindly apologize to Colonel Ikonenko this instant, and if indeed you have drugged the soldiery, I would ask you to bring them to a state of consciousness with all due despatch.

MAN. I've never been so bullied in all my endless life ! Why should I apologize to Ikonenko ? He called me names, and I'm very sensitive indeed. As for the soldiers, they're asleep, not drugged.

DESMOND. Then wake them up. If they sleep any longer they'll miss their tea. As for Ikonenko, I must appeal to what sense of honour you have to realize that there's a great difference between an officer doing his duty and a fellow assing around with live bullets inside him and refusing to lie down.

MAN. No, I won't apologize. I'm sulking.

DESMOND. In that case, I have no alternative but to place you under arrest pending investigation. (*To his colleagues.*) Do you agree with me ?

WESLEY. I guess so, but I don't like it. Say, how do you do it ? You'd have had a great future in Chicago in the 'twenties.

MAN (*laughs*). I'd have had a great future ! Splendid muddle of tenses for a mere mortal ! What you mean to say is, I had a great past. (*In a faultless American accent.*) I was always at Al Capone's shoulder, and I was with Dillinger when he died.

WESLEY. That I don't believe.

DESMOND. The next thing you'll be saying in your damned irresponsible way is that you were there when Cæsar crossed the Rubicon.

MAN. No, I wasn't. But then I didn't like Cæsar personally, and when I don't like people, they've had it. What are you doing?

(DESMOND *rings the bell*.)

DESMOND. Ringing for Sergeant Daniels.

MAN. But you saw what happened before. The men are all asleep.

DESMOND. They'll come if I ring.

AIMÉ. Tell us about the castle.

DESMOND. I advise you not to talk to the fellow.

AIMÉ. I want to know. You see, I think we ought to arrest him, but I don't think we can.

MAN. Bravo. The castle? Yes. I'll take you there if you're very, very good.

DESMOND. If I go, I go alone.

MAN. You won't get in. You see, it is not a castle like any other. It is a castle touched by magic.

(*A very beautiful, but very prim* A.T.S. GIRL *appears at the door*.)

GIRL. You rang, sir?

MAN (*horrified*). You? Here?

DESMOND. Who the devil are you?

GIRL. Private Donovan. Your new driver, sir. Reporting for duty.

DESMOND. I told you they'd come if I rang. But look here, what's happened to Private Nash?

GIRL. Went sick, sir.

MAN (*violent*). Why did you come here? Just as I was getting on so well!

DESMOND. Donovan. D'you know this man?

GIRL (*sadly*). Yes, sir.

DESMOND. Who is he?

GIRL. I've known him for years, sir.

DESMOND. Eh? Where?

GIRL. Everywhere.

DESMOND. For years? How many years?

GIRL. About six thousand.

DESMOND. Donovan, I warn you. I'm in no mood for jollity.

GIRL. I'm telling the truth, sir. I've brought the car.

DESMOND. What for?

GIRL. To drive you to the castle.

DESMOND. I didn't order it.

GIRL. You were going to, though, sir.

DESMOND. But you haven't answered my first question yet. Who is this fellow?

GIRL. He's an old enemy. (*Fresh thought.*) You'll have plenty of time to find out, sir, at the castle.

MAN (*sad*). Are you coming too?

GIRL. I'm driving you.

MAN. There goes my fun.

AIMÉ. Fun? What fun?

GIRL (*seeing* IKONENKO, *who is still in a state of collapse*). Oh, the poor colonel! (*She takes him in her lap, and rocks him, administering smelling salts which she produces from her pocket.*)

DESMOND. Donovan, will you kindly put the Colonel down, and inform me first of all about yourself and then about this man.

GIRL (*smiles*). How are your dogs, sir, Ranger, Thunderbolt and Black Havoc?

DESMOND. Extremely fit, thank you, by the latest reports. How do you know about them?

GIRL. Ah, Colonel Breitenspiegel, you were wrong to trust your wife's psychiatrist.

WESLEY. Why?

GIRL. He's taking advantage of your absence. He took your wife to the Stork Club last night, and then——

WESLEY (*rising with a howl*). What!

MAN. Spoilsport!

GIRL. And you, Colonel Frappot. It was sinful of you to tell the Mayor that your wife was living with a haulage-contractor while you are living with an actress. It's true that you live with an actress, but your wife is utterly faithful to this day, and lives in hopes . . .

AIMÉ (*unsurprised*). One tells little lies to appease one's conscience—and then, my wife's fidelity has always seemed to me so embarrassingly un-French.

GIRL. Or just embarrassing?

AIMÉ. Or just embarrassing.

IKONENKO (*stirs*). Where am I ?

GIRL (*going to him*). You've been a bad boy, Colonel Ikonenko, shooting at a man.

IKONENKO. Is he dead ?

GIRL. No.

IKONENKO (*writhing*). I have failed ! I have failed !

GIRL. No, dear Colonel, you have not.

IKONENKO. My life is finished. I must go to Moscow and confess.

GIRL. You're coming to the castle with us.

IKONENKO. The castle . . .

GIRL. Yes, to visit the Sleeping Beauty.

DESMOND. What's that ?

GIRL. Yes, sir, it's the castle where the Sleeping Beauty has been asleep for a hundred years.

DESMOND. Donovan, I warn you. I'm sure you're an excellent driver, but I won't have romancing.

WESLEY. Romancing !

AIMÉ. La Belle Au Bois Dormant.

DESMOND. What ?

AIMÉ. The Beauty of the Sleeping Forest.

IKONENKO. Tchaikovsky.

AIMÉ. But then, who are you, Miss Donovan ?

DESMOND. Just call her plain Donovan, Aimé. She's in uniform.

AIMÉ. She is too beautiful for such familiarity, at least at the beginning. . . . Dear Miss Donovan, please tell us who you are.

(*The* GIRL *looks round for a moment, in a quandary.*)

MAN (*hurt*). Might as well tell them now. The harm's done. Thanks to you, you silly immortal bitch.

GIRL (*smiles radiantly*). In the visible world I have many names. In pre-history, I was the angel charged with the painful duty of chasing Adam and Eve out of the Garden of Eden. (*Racked with remorse.*) Oh, if only I had been there first, I could have warned them . . .

MAN (*mocking*). But you weren't.

GIRL (*sad*). I wasn't. And in the world of dreams and legends, they call me the Good Fairy.

AIMÉ (*softly*). And what do we call you ?

GIRL (*with a shrug and a charming smile*). Donovan.

MAN (*piqued*). Well . . . is nobody going to ask me who I am ?

DESMOND. We have done so consistently, sir. I can only take it as a reflection on your character that you have to be provoked into a confession by Donovan's good example. (*Aside.*) Full marks, Donovan.

MAN (*scoffing*). Good example, my magic wand ! I, too, have many names in the foolish world of things and facts and figures. In pre-history, I won my first victory over Donovan, in that same Garden of Eden where she first learned what she was up against. Yes. (*Vindictive.*) I was the Serpent who gave Eve the forbidden apple. The devil was absent. He didn't realize the importance of the occasion. Since then, Donovan and I have been struggling for the driving reins of this ramshackle carriage they call humanity —a carriage in which all the living recline and jostle each other on the rough road they travel. I can tempt, and so can Donovan, and you, gentlemen, are our battleground. You and Eve and the Sleeping Beauty, and all the peoples and dreams of the world. (*Suddenly agonized.*) And you have the wonderful possibility of choosing . . .

AIMÉ. Choosing ? Why do you think that should give us such pleasure ? Personally, I welcome an escape into that world of dreams and legends where Donovan loses her prosaic name and becomes the Good Fairy. You did not tell, mon serpent, what is your name in that sweeter world ?

MAN. Me ? (*A peal of laughter, followed by an elaborate gesture.*) Silly boy, I'm the Wicked Fairy !

CURTAIN.

ACT II.

Within the castle. When the curtain rises, all is dark. All that can be heard is a sound, which may be music, of a deep, mysterious and atmospheric sort. Trees rustle and sigh. The noise of a car can be heard. Brakes are applied. Doors slam. A jumble of voices.

WESLEY'S VOICE. Come on, in here.

AIMÉ'S VOICE. Ow!

DESMOND'S VOICE. What is it? Oh, drat!

IKONENKO'S VOICE. A step, two steps, ai!

(A torch appears.)

WESLEY (*overawed*). Can you see anything?

(As the COLONELS *file in, he shines his torch on the set, which reveals nothing but a forbidding screen of sagging gauzes.)*

Kind of eerie.

WICKED FAIRY. It's what you asked for.

DESMOND. Can we have some light?

WICKED FAIRY. How do you expect me to produce light?

DESMOND. Magic.

WICKED FAIRY. So you do admit of such a thing?

DESMOND. I'm not one to look a gift horse in the mouth.

(The front of the stage becomes lighter.)

IKONENKO (*eyes gleaming*). This looks the kind of castle where jewels lie hidden.

AIMÉ. Do I hear the people's representative hoping to find jewels?

WICKED FAIRY. The people's representative stole a diamond-studded watch from a German duchess.

IKONENKO. It's a lie. I exchanged it against a Soviet cuckoo-clock.

ACT II (*from left to right*) MOIRA LISTER, PETER USTINOV, EUGENE DECKERS AND GWEN CHERRELL.

Photograph by Denis De Marney

AIMÉ. Where will you take us from here ?

WICKED FAIRY. You're boys at heart, the four of you. You'd much rather explore than be shown anything, wouldn't you ?

WESLEY. Sure. Speaking for myself.

WICKED FAIRY. Go on, then. I'll show you all you want to know when you have found nothing.

WESLEY. Come on, fellers.

DESMOND. Where are you going to be ? You won't leave us here alone ?

WICKED FAIRY. We won't. I just want a word with Donovan.

DESMOND. Have I your word ?

GOOD FAIRY (*entering*). You have my word.

DESMOND. Good enough for me, Donovan.

IKONENKO. I shall try the floorboards . . .

(*They go.*)

GOOD FAIRY. You want a word with me ? Why ?

WICKED FAIRY. I hardly know where to begin. That's odd for me, isn't it ?

GOOD FAIRY. Are you trying to be sincere ?

WICKED FAIRY (*looking away from her*). Isn't it embarrassing ?

(*Pause.*)

You see, in a strange way, these four idiots have touched me . . .

GOOD FAIRY. What game are you playing now ?

WICKED FAIRY. My dear child, if I was playing a game, I'd do it in the usual way. I'm too old, too hidebound, for innovations. (*Softer.*) I mean what I say with all the very limited sincerity at my disposal.

GOOD FAIRY. Why should these four have touched you, when you have ridden roughshod over the dead, and even worse, the dying ? When throughout our immortality you have spent your sleepless existence gloating over misery and vice ?

WICKED FAIRY. That's just it. I'm beginning to tire. (*Pause.*) Oh, Donovan, if you knew, if you could guess . . .

GOOD FAIRY. What ?

WICKED FAIRY. How I am dying to do a good deed !

GOOD FAIRY. Ssh ! (*Nervous.*) Be careful what you say . . .

WICKED FAIRY. I've become quite reckless. I sometimes

can't bear to do the obvious. I'm such an expert in evil that there's no challenge any more. I dream of new worlds to conquer. I dream of one day saving a life . . . or at least of upholding a fidelity. Can you understand ?

GOOD FAIRY. Too well ! If you knew how the mawkishness of inhuman kindness had begun to pall ! Perfection is a stagnant thing. Oh, Serpent, I'm longing to be bad. Just for once.

WICKED FAIRY. Now I could almost forget who I am, and fall in love.

GOOD FAIRY. With me ? Surely not.

WICKED FAIRY. Yes. One kiss would bring me peace for centuries. I could drain a little goodness from your lips, and it would linger through the years, tingeing the mind with sweetness, and making a memory of that empty space I call my heart.

GOOD FAIRY. And I could sense the poison of your tongue. I would be stung by the sadness of the world, and drown for a moment in the savage pallor of your eyes. Then I would taste of that bitter thing they call reality.

(*They are standing very close to each other.*)

Dare we ?

WICKED FAIRY (*heartcry*). No !

GOOD FAIRY (*breaking away*). It was a silly game to have played.

WICKED FAIRY. If the extremes collided they would crush the whole of life between them. (*Quiet and bitter.*) We have our duty.

GOOD FAIRY. How I envy mortals.

WICKED FAIRY. They can choose between us. We have no choice.

GOOD FAIRY. We must return to our predestined positions.

(*Pause.*)

WICKED FAIRY (*gentle*). Donovan . . .

GOOD FAIRY. Mm ?

WICKED FAIRY. Would we be failing in our duty if we agreed not to interfere for once ?

GOOD FAIRY. What are you thinking of ?

WICKED FAIRY. The four idiots.

GOOD FAIRY. They are good men.

WICKED FAIRY. Idiots.

Good Fairy. You mean, if when we show them the Beauty, we let them try to awaken her love, each in his own way, without our influence ?

Wicked Fairy. Yes.

Good Fairy. Is that possible ? What could men do without good and evil ? They too would lose the joy of strategy, the possibility of choice.

Wicked Fairy. But love is stronger than choice. Love has made laughing stocks of us both. Remember how we struggled over Romeo and Juliet, Paolo and Francesca, the whole damned cohort of star-kissed lovers who escaped from us into a blameless and enviable death ? Love is our only common enemy.

Good Fairy. Love is my friend.

Wicked Fairy. Carnal love ?

Good Fairy. Spiritual love.

Wicked Fairy. And the love that leads to suicide ? No, my dear, we don't know where we stand with love. After all, it has even affected both of us. . . . You are the conscience, I, the primitive desire. We may struggle for the heart——

Good Fairy.—but it is a battle neither of us can ever win.

Wicked Fairy (*suffering*). That is something these poor mortals must never know. That is our ghastly secret . . .

Good Fairy. But can we trust ourselves not to interfere ?

Wicked Fairy. You mean, can you trust me ?

Good Fairy (*shy*). Yes . . .

Wicked Fairy. I'll try to behave. I can't say more than that.

Good Fairy (*tender*). No, you can't . . .

(*She makes an instinctive movement towards him, but breaks away when the voice of the* Colonels *are heard. The four* Colonels *return.*)

Wesley. This place is like a maze.

Aimé. Of what period is the architecture ?

Wicked Fairy (*abstracted, gazing tenderly at the* Good Fairy). Modern . . .

Aimé. What ?

Wicked Fairy (*recovering*). Oh, I beg your pardon. Comparatively modern. Thirteenth century. It was built by Otho, First Grand Duke of Burg zu Burg-Burg von Herzogenburg. A charming man.

Good Fairy. A brute.

WICKED FAIRY. His successor, Willibald, was a relatively weedy boy of seven foot two, who was a perfect pest.

GOOD FAIRY. He relieved me of a great deal of worry.

WICKED FAIRY. Yes, he was the first man to fit a primitive equivalent of a Yale lock on to a chastity belt.

IKONENKO. May we visit some other rooms ?

WICKED FAIRY. You will do better. You will see the Sleeping Beauty. She will wake up soon.

AIMÉ. But the legend says she will wake only when Prince Charming kisses her, at the end of a hundred years.

WICKED FAIRY. This will be a temporary awakening for your benefit. She will have to sleep again later. That is—unless *you* succeed.

IKONENKO. Succeed ?

WESLEY. What are we waiting for ? Is she yummy ?

WICKED FAIRY. Is she what ?

WESLEY. Has she got " it " ?

WICKED FAIRY. What ?

DESMOND. Is she personable ?

AIMÉ. Est-ce qu'elle a du chien ?

WICKED FAIRY. Du chien ?

IKONENKO. Is she sexually attractive ?

DESMOND. He's damned coarse, this fellow.

WICKED FAIRY. Now, I must ask for complete silence from you gentlemen. The next step is fraught with technical difficulties. No time to explain now. . . . Donovan !

(*The two* FAIRIES *stand with their backs to the audience and raise their arms. As they do so, the stage grows dark, to notes of a glacial music. When the lights come up again, they reveal the proscenium of a Court Theatre of the early nineteenth century. It is elaborate and golden, with all the attendant symbolism of this type of erection. Small Royal box,* L. *In it the King and Queen, asleep. The King leans drunkenly over the parapet. The Queen, lies back, sleeping and aghast. Box on the right, empty. On the stage, a fantastic and elaborate bed, in which lies the veiled and fragile figure of the* SLEEPING BEAUTY. *The music stops.*)

IKONENKO (*suddenly filled with wonder*). It is exactly as I had always imagined it.

AIMÉ. No, it is as I have often seen it in illustrations, and therefore not as I had imagined it. The French genius is the genius of mistrust.

DESMOND. Plenty of time for philosophizing later. Donovan, put me in the picture.

GOOD FAIRY. Yes, sir. We are in the Court Theatre of King Florestan the Twenty-fourth, which was added to the castle in 1816. In spite of the Queen, whom you see sleeping up there, he had a . . . a morganatic arrangement with an actress.

WICKED FAIRY (*laughs mockingly*). He liked to call himself a King. He was only a Grand Duke really.

GOOD FAIRY. It happened a hundred years ago to-day. It was Aurora's birthday, and I was among the guests. My friend here, Carabosse——

DESMOND. Who ?

WICKED FAIRY. Me. Carabosse. Not my real name. A kind of nom-de-fée.

DESMOND. I see. Go on, Donovan.

GOOD FAIRY. Carabosse was, for obvious reasons, not in the King's engagement book, and he was not invited to the Christening——

IKONENKO. But any child knows this story !

DESMOND. Any child may, but there are still a few colonels who do not. Donovan.

GOOD FAIRY. He determined to be revenged, and therefore uttered a terrible curse on this house.

WESLEY. What do you know ?

GOOD FAIRY. The curse was that should Aurora ever prick herself with anything sharp, she would die. Naturally, we kept everything remotely sharp away from her. It worked, until this terrible day. (*Self-effacing.*) In my infinite innocence——

WICKED FAIRY (*with a cackle*). Bravo !

GOOD FAIRY. In my infinite innocence, I wrote a play, a pastoral piece in rhyming couplets, gentle and sweet as the first ray of dawn——

WICKED FAIRY. Sickly as a piece of Turkish delight.

GOOD FAIRY. In it I foolishly placed a spinning-wheel. However, this was a play, a little diversion, a make-believe, an unreality. The needle was made of twisted silver paper, and could not hurt a fly. (*Remorseful.*) I was not to know that the Chamberlain, who is now asleep in the wings—I was not to know that he was unreliable. He was charged with

the stage management, and he substituted the paper needle
with a——

WESLEY (*emotional*). Oh no, don't tell me!

GOOD FAIRY. With a real one.

WESLEY (*suffering*). Oh no, oh no.

GOOD FAIRY. The rest of the story must be clear to you.

IKONENKO (*on his usual warning note*). It is not exactly as it
is in the ballet.

GOOD FAIRY. Very few things are. Aurora pricked herself
in the third act, when the entire court was charmed by her exqui-
site purity. She died. I brought her back to life, but she fell into
a deep sleep, and here she lies . . .

WICKED FAIRY. The rest is up to you.

WESLEY. What can we do?

WICKED FAIRY. Win her heart. Tempt her, as I tempted
Eve—only I warn you, your task will be more difficult, as she is not
yet married.

WESLEY. She'll never look at us.

WICKED FAIRY. Why shouldn't she?

WESLEY. Well, Look at me, for instance. *And* I need glasses
to read.

WICKED FAIRY. Don't you think that after a perfumed
existence, in which beauty has become a commonplace, a myopic
man might be a rarity, and consequently a thing of loveliness?

WESLEY. What? Me, a thing of loveliness? That's effeminate
talk. I'll knock you down if you——

(WESLEY *adopts a threatening attitude. The* WICKED FAIRY *raises
his hand, and* WESLEY *is frozen into belligerent immobility. As
the others stare at* WESLEY, *the* WICKED FAIRY *continues unper-
turbed.*)

WICKED FAIRY. Or Aurora may prefer the sparse carrotty
whiskers of Colonel Rinder-Sparrow, or the garlic-flavoured
breath of Colonel Frappot, or the porous nose of Colonel Ikonenko.
These attributes are rare as radium in fairyland.

(*The* GOOD FAIRY *sees* WESLEY.)

GOOD FAIRY (*annoyed*). Carabosse!

(*She blows on* WESLEY *gently, and he is released from the spell. The
others gather round him.*)

DESMOND. Are you all right, old chap ?

WICKED FAIRY (*to* GOOD FAIRY). May they go and look at her, do you think ?

GOOD FAIRY (*to* WICKED FAIRY : *schoolmasters discussing the future of the boys*). I see no harm in it, so long as they don't touch her.

WICKED FAIRY. No, they mustn't touch her. (*To the* COLONELS.) All right, go and look at her, but don't touch her.

(*The* FOUR COLONELS *clamber on to the stage.*)

GOOD FAIRY. What shall we do next ?

WICKED FAIRY (*cruelly*). Why do you ask me ?

GOOD FAIRY. Evil always has the initiative.

(WESLEY *emits the conventional low whistle.*)

You see. I am only the one who prevents you from achieving your aims.

WICKED FAIRY. Sometimes.

GOOD FAIRY (*sad*). Sometimes . . .

WICKED FAIRY. Well, as a matter of fact, I have a brainwave.

GOOD FAIRY (*full of doubt*). Mm. Let's hear it.

WICKED FAIRY. We will continue with the theatrical performance after an interval of a hundred years. We will give a performance couched deeply in the Colonels' imagination.

GOOD FAIRY. I don't understand.

WICKED FAIRY. Look at them up there, prowling round her like wolves round the sheeps' pen. To them she is the ideal. They all see her in different ways. Only lust is common to them all.

GOOD FAIRY (*suffering*). Yes.

WICKED FAIRY. Then let's bring Aurora back to momentary life, and——

WESLEY (*calling from the stage*). Hey, Fairies, I'm in love.

WICKED FAIRY. What did I tell you ?

DESMOND. She's damned attractive. A lovely, fair-haired English rose.

WESLEY. Fair ? She's got red hair, like flame.

AIMÉ. Red ? She's the type of dark Mediterranean beauty like one finds in Marseilles.

IKONENKO. Dark ? A typical distortion. She is flaxen, like the farm girls in the Ukraine. Her face betrays deep convictions and a desire for immediate motherhood.

WICKED FAIRY.   You are all in love with her ?

WESLEY (*with boundless enthusiasm*).   Sure !

DESMOND.   I must say she strikes a chord in me that has not been struck since my cadet days.

AIMÉ.   I don't know whether I have the capacity for a love which is free from the selfish manœuvres of a carnal attachment. However, I am not a fool.   I would like to sleep with her.

IKONENKO.   I have already made my position clear in this matter.

WICKED FAIRY.   Very well.   But first, gentlemen . . . (*He goes up to the centre of the stage, and beckons the* COLONELS *to gather round him.   Secretive.*)   A word in your ear about . . .

(*The* WICKED FAIRY *points to the* BEAUTY.   *He appears about to impart a confidence to the* COLONELS, *who cluster round him in the centre of the stage, by the footlights.   Suddenly the curtain-within-a-curtain falls, leaving the* COLONELS *outside.   The* WICKED FAIRY *cackles with laughter.   The* COLONELS *are caught unawares and are angry.*)

WESLEY.   Hey, what's happened to the girl ?

WICKED FAIRY.   You shall see her, if you behave. (*The Colonels struggle to penetrate the curtains.*) No, you can't get through there, I'm sorry.

(*The* COLONELS *come down from the stage.*)

AIMÉ.   What do you wish us to do ?

WICKED FAIRY.   You're interested, aren't you ?

AIMÉ.   Very.   My life has been an experiment.   I have explored the byways of the senses and almost arrived at a conclusion.   The last thing I wanted was to arrive at a conclusion.

GOOD FAIRY.   You have searched too hard, and reached the wrong conclusion !

AIMÉ.   That we are animals tortured by a thinking brain ? That there is no lingering beauty, that it is a momentary flame, sweet, but with its very sweetness soured in advance by the knowledge of its filthy aftertaste ?   No, my dear, existence is a shocking business.   And existence is love.

WICKED FAIRY.   Go and prove it.   But first, become the character you always hoped to be in your child's heart.

AIMÉ. I have no illusions. The only character I always hoped to be is myself.

WICKED FAIRY. Have you no favourite period in history at least ?

AIMÉ. Ah, yes. That is different. The turn of the eighteenth century, when France was innundated with the sun, reflected off her sovereign's pride.

WICKED FAIRY. Will you go first ?

AIMÉ. Where to ?

WICKED FAIRY. To act your love to your ideal.

AIMÉ (*falters*). Here ?

WICKED FAIRY. On the stage ! Now ! Go into the wings, you will find all there to fit your most private dreams.

AIMÉ. And she will appear ?

WICKED FAIRY. As your ideal. As your hope. As what you left behind when you first knew a woman !

(*After a moment of hesitation, AIMÉ submits to temptation, and runs into the wings.*)

Music !

GOOD FAIRY (*urgent*). Oh, don't wake the conductor ! He only confuses the orchestra when he's conscious. He's so bad, the poor darling.

WICKED FAIRY. What do you suggest ?

GOOD FAIRY. For the eighteenth century ? Wake Herr Doktor Gimpel, the Harpist, Herr Doktor Straubel, the Flautist, and—Herr Professor Kampff, the Violinist.

WICKED FAIRY (*calling into the orchestra pit*). Herr Doktor Gimpel, Herr Doktor Straubel, Herr Professor Kampff ! Music of the eighteenth century, please ! Hey Presto. Hey Lento, Hey Allegro—Ma Non Troppo !

(*Lights appear under the protective palm leaves. The lights in the theatre dim. The footlights go up. The three instruments begin to tune up.*)

DESMOND. I say, what *is* going on ? Are we to be treated to a theatrical performance ? And if so, why ?

WICKED FAIRY. It will be your turn next.

DESMOND. Mine ?

WICKED FAIRY. Yes. You too will become upon the stage your secret self, in quest of your ideal. Now sit down.

WESLEY.   Where ?

WICKED FAIRY.   Here.   (*He indicates one of the boxes at the side of the stage.*)   I will sit here—(*He indicates the box on the opposite side*)—and you, my dear, here.   (*He fetches a gilt chair for the* GOOD FAIRY, *and places it in front of his own.*)

GOOD FAIRY.   How kind of you to fetch me a chair.

WICKED FAIRY.   So much of my time is spent with the upper classes.

(*The music begins.*)

IKONENKO.   I don't understand what this performance will prove.

WICKED FAIRY.   Would you mind keeping quiet please ! after all, you are in the theatre, gentlemen.   Pray silence while we see the naked soul of a certain Aimé Frappot chasing the elusive bird which flutters in his heart.   And may he catch it !

WESLEY.   Just before we start, is this some form of psychiatry?

(*The* WICKED FAIRY *silences him with an impatient gesture.   The curtain-within-a-curtain rises slowly.   The sketchy set shows an interior of* 1700.   THE BEAUTY *sits at a dressing table, making up her face.   She is in corsets.   Her black hair flows down her back, while her wig is on a wig-stand.*)

DESMOND (*whisper*).   Who's that ?

GOOD FAIRY (*enchanted*).   The Beauty.   How lovely she looks in that costume.

IKONENKO (*loud*).   That's not the Beauty !

WICKED FAIRY.   Of course it is, idiot.   Aimé's Beauty.

BEAUTY (*as the music stops*).   Heigh-ho.   It is but eleven o'clock in the morning, and already I am awake, for when a woman of the town must choose a husband, it is wise to rise early. (*She powders her face.*)

IKONENKO.   Eleven o'clock is late, not early.

'VICKED FAIRY.   Sssh ! Give your colleague a chance.

BEAUTY.   Husband ! What a tedious thing is man when he is called by the vile name of husband !—And yet, were there no husband, the little lapses that women of the town dote upon would lack of savour.   (*Laughs.*)   Yes, I have ribboned bonnets, a wardrobe as fine as the richest in Paris, periwigs and toys and baubles, pretty little dogs, black boys to serve chocolate, a Dutch milliner, an Italian dancing master, and all that elegance could wish. (*Melancholy.*) Yet now I lack a lover. But first, a husband, for without a husband to deceive, a lover's an empty pleasure. But hist, one comes. I shall dissemble.

(AIMÉ *enters, immensely romantic in the costume of the period, and winks at the audience.*)

AIMÉ (*bowing deeply*). Mademoiselle, methought this to be a coffee-house.

BEAUTY. A coffee-house, sir ? A coffee-house, sir ? How came you by this notion ?

AIMÉ. I know not, and it matters less. (*Aside.*) I had observed her through the window while in quest of a coffee-house. My taste for coffee was dispersed.

BEAUTY. A bold gallant, too good for husbanding. I shall pretend to hate him. (*To* AIMÉ.) Sir, that you were in search of a coffee-house, I doubt not. That you have found one, however, I doubt much. Now there's nothing in a man so odious as a mind which is ever, like a butterfly, fluttering hither and thither, from purpose to purpose, and therefore, sir, if you hope for my respect, I pray you turn about and *find* a coffee-house.

AIMÉ (*aside*). Which means she loves me. (*To her.*) If I were sure, Mademoiselle, that the coffee-house would hold such charms as these, still I would not go, for any journey would be irksome that carried the traveller away from you, and then, what fool would engender your respect, and not tarry to enjoy it ?

BEAUTY (*aside*). I doubt that it is my respect he wants. Yes, alas, he is too good for husband, and too soon for lover ! (*To him.*) Are you not afraid to incur my wrath, sir ?

AIMÉ. No, Mademoiselle, for it is à la mode to hate in public those you would tumble behind locked doors.

BEAUTY (*aside*). He speaks like a gentleman indeed. (*To him.*) Then I, sir, am not of the rule, for when I hate, I hate, and there's an end to't.

AIMÉ (*aside*). She loves me more with every phrase she utters. (*To her.*) Then, madam, I am here to a double purpose.

BEAUTY. Nay, nay, why do you call me " madam " now ?

AIMÉ. You have a short wind for raillery, madam, which betokens that you are but lately brought to bed by a husband, and have not yet wearied of his palsied face upon your pillow.

BEAUTY (*aside*). Now could I love him. Were't better to admit

I am a maid, or, sighing, say, " Alas, sir, what you suppose is true.
I have a husband."

AIMÉ (*aside*). See, she sighs and moans, and each heaving of
those twin rotundities doth seem to beckon me.

BEAUTY. Sir, I am indeed cursed with husband, as hideous a
vaporous wretch as was ever purg'd by physick, for indeed all he
touches, or breathes upon—or fondles—has upon it the cloying
stench of Pharmacy.

AIMÉ. Ha !

BEAUTY (*aside*). I have affected him.

AIMÉ (*aside*). I will approach her.

BEAUTY (*aside*). Heigh-ho, how sweet is the lot of woman
when it is not miserable. (*To him.*) Have you done prowling, sir ?

AIMÉ (*aside*). So ? She is impatient ?

BEAUTY (*aside*). This then is the calm, which, preceding the
storm, doth make the storm so very much more enjoyable.

(AIMÉ *seizes her. The other* COLONELS *rise from their seats in
astonishment.*)

BEAUTY. I shall scream, sir !

AIMÉ. Untruss, ma'am, untruss !

BEAUTY. I shall box your ears, sir !

AIMÉ. You conspire to add to their delight !

BEAUTY. I shall black your eye, sir !

AIMÉ. And surround your image with a coronet of stars !

BEAUTY. I shall smack your cheek, sir !

AIMÉ. To aid a lover's blush !

BEAUTY. I shall pummel you, sir !

AIMÉ. And I shall think it is the beating of your heart !

BEAUTY. Help, help ! (*As he has almost stolen the fatal kiss.*)
I am a virgin, sir !

DESMOND. Good God !

AIMÉ (*releasing her abruptly*). How ? How's this ?

(*The other* COLONELS *relax and go back to their seats.*)

BEAUTY (*pouting*). I lied . . . a little lie, sir, to fan the flame
of ardour.

AIMÉ (*with aloof savagery*). You call it a little lie, miss, to create
a husband i' the mind as full of good, solid, husbandly vices as the
million others of the cursed band ? You call it a little lie to drive

me on in the hope of theft, to find that you are ownerless ? You call it a little lie to flatter me by breathing scandal of an imaginary spouse ?

BEAUTY (*aside*). How he glowers ! I must appease him, for he is a handsome enough coxcomb, and may have his uses. I will sing awhile. (*Aloud*). La-la-la. Fol-de-rol-lol.

GOOD FAIRY. Oh, thank goodness.

IKONENKO (*exploding*). That's not the Beauty ! Where are her motherly virtues ?

DESMOND. I certainly can't call this lass innocent. Is that what he sees in her ?

WESLEY. She sure knows her way around.

GOOD FAIRY (*sighs*). Yes, that's what he sees in her. But the fatal kiss was avoided, that's all I care about.

DESMOND. But Donovan, are you *sure* it's the same girl as I saw sleeping up there ? Admittedly, there is a superficial resemblance, but——

GOOD FAIRY. It's the same girl, sir. You will see her in a different light when your turn comes.

IKONENKO. Have they finished ? Has he failed ?

GOOD FAIRY. Yes. Carabosse. (*Suddenly jumps up.*) Where is he ?

DESMOND. Who ?

GOOD FAIRY. Carabosse !

DESMOND. He's gone !

(*Not at all. He enters on the stage, as the very description which the* BEAUTY *gave of her imaginary husband.*)

WICKED FAIRY. So soon abroad, my love, my chick, my doll ? And has't thou drunk thy chocolate yet, and hast thou learned thy minuet and little songs, and hast thou pretty things to tell me ? Hm ? Eh ?

GOOD FAIRY (*heartcry*). I knew he'd have to interfere !

WICKED FAIRY (*Aside, to* GOOD FAIRY). My nature was too strong for me !

GOOD FAIRY. You haven't beaten me yet !

(*The* GOOD FAIRY *runs off* R.)

AIMÉ. Oons ! It is her father !

WICKED FAIRY. Zounds ! I am her husband !

BEAUTY. My husband, say you ?

AIMÉ. How ? (*Aside.*) Thus was her lie no lie at all, but a strategy to draw out my anguish, and with my anguish, my delight !

BEAUTY (*aside*). That I have no husband I am sure, though I'm sure I'm eager to acquire one. This old fool is ugly enough— and blind enough, for if he mistake me for his wife now, he will again, or I'll see to't.

WICKED FAIRY. Madam, I pray you, tell me who is this gallant who appears to be studying the wall with such grave and scholarly attention ?

BEAUTY (*with deep disdain*). That is my eunuch, sir.

WICKED FAIRY. An eunuch, madam ?

BEAUTY. Yes, an eunuch from the Ottoman realm.

WICKED FAIRY (*aside*). Yea, straight from the ottoman, I'll warrant. Her hair is all unkempt, while he doth avert his eyes to cover his confusion. I'll talk with him. (*Aloud.*) Sir ! Sir, I say !

AIMÉ (*falsetto*). Sir, I am your honour's most obliged, most devoted servant.

WICKED FAIRY (*aside*). There's truth in't then. (*Aloud.*) And I your's, sir, I assure you.

(*The* BEAUTY *pretends to faint.*)

BEAUTY. Oh ! I faint ! Help !

WICKED FAIRY. My knicknack ! My bee ! My grouse ! My pigeon ! My widgeon ! What ails thee ?

BEAUTY. A lack of breath, sir.

WICKED FAIRY. Which physick declares to be no more than an over-excess of vacuum.

BEAUTY. And a swimming of the brain, sir.

WICKED FAIRY. Ah ! A case of innundation of the mentality.

BEAUTY. And a stopping of the heart, sir.

WICKED FAIRY. Or lack of movement in the sentimental regions.

BEAUTY. And a freezing of the hand, sir.

WICKED FAIRY. Yes, yes, an insufficiency of manual torpor.

BEAUTY. And a shivering of the limb, sir.

WICKED FAIRY. Cardinal ! Capital ! An instability of the pedestrian organ ! Attend me, my nightingale, my owlkin, my nightjar. I'll fetch thee medicine straight.

(*He goes. Immediately the* BEAUTY *and* AIMÉ *fly into each other's arms.   They are about to kiss, when the* GOOD FAIRY *enters, disguised.*)

GOOD FAIRY.   Hold!
AIMÉ (*out of character, faltering*).   Jeanette . . .
BEAUTY.   What name was that?

(AIMÉ *releases her.*)

Thy wife?
AIMÉ.   My mistress.
BEAUTY.   How?   Thou hast a mistress—and a wife?   How have I been deceived!
GOOD FAIRY.   Thy victims grow younger, chick, which is a sign o' the approach of hoary winter in a man.
AIMÉ.   Hoary is well said, ma'am.   For a man is like a ship which leaves the harbour.   First is he set loose upon the calm waters of life, and spends his innocence in the mole's embrace. Then he comes to man's estate, and senses the ocean's subtle billows at the harbour mouth, and then, with age, his horizon does grow wider, until, out of sight of land, he believes the whole wild wilderness of water to be his, and all the great regiment of women in the world for him alone.   There's the irony o' the world.   When too young to know, he loves a woman, cruel and playful.   When too old to be able, he loves the whole cursed sex.   (*With dignified pathos.*)   He has lost sight of land . . .
BEAUTY.   Nay, then, sir, I will not love thee, for be one of ten or twenty is to be in the fashion, but to be loved as one of an entire sex verges upon the indiscriminate.   I'll none of your waves and billows, sir, your seascapes and marine fancies.   I am of the land, sir, and with that send you packing.   (*Aside.*)   How handsome does his grief render him, his brow arched in noble melancholy, his eye upcast in pain.   Now could I love him indeed.
AIMÉ (*aside*).   Ah, how a refusal should spur me on!   And yet——
GOOD FAIRY.   Come then, sir, content yourself with a well-remembered face.   The lines of sorrow upon it are your own.

(AIMÉ *smiles at her.*)

GOOD FAIRY.   Cans't see thy signature upon my cheeks, thy seal upon my lips?   And cans't see thy younger self reflected in my eye?

AIMÉ.   Thou art like an old song, but ill-remembered.

GOOD FAIRY.   And quick to learn again ?

(*She holds out her hands to* AIMÉ, *who seizes them and kisses them.
The* BEAUTY *bursts into tears.   The* WICKED FAIRY *enters.*)

WICKED FAIRY.   Here's medicine, my cake, my bun, my
sweetmeat . . .

(*He senses the situation, loses all sense of character as well as his
temper, and shouts—*)

Curtain !   Bring it down !   The play is over !

(*Consternation.   The curtain falls.*)

DESMOND.   What d'you make of it ?

WESLEY.   I didn't understand his motivation.

IKONENKO.   He treated her like a swine.

WESLEY.   Why did he want her to be married ?

DESMOND.   He's always given me the impression of a fellow
who's a bit sick of women, but who can't leave them alone.

WESLEY.   Yeah, but that doesn't explain why he throws over
a girl as fresh as that for the second dame.   She was one whole
lot older.

DESMOND.   Yes.   She was a bit long in the tooth.   What did he
call her ?   Jeanette ?

WICKED FAIRY (*looking through the curtains*).   Colonel Rinder-
Sparrow.   How do you see yourself ?

DESMOND.   Eh ?

WICKED FAIRY.   What is the embodiment of your romantic
self ?

DESMOND.   Goodness knows.

WESLEY.   You probably see yourself as a golden retriever.

DESMOND.   No need to be rude about dogs, Wesley.   They're
finer souls than you or I.

WESLEY.   O.K.   Go up there as one.   See the Beauty as a
pekingese.

DESMOND.   Just a minute.   There was a bloke who always
fascinated me.

WICKED FAIRY.   Who ?

DESMOND.   When I was small, and allowed to stay up late with
the grown-ups, there was a family portrait just opposite my chair,

Photograph by Denis De Marney

ACT II (*from left to right*) MOIRA LISTER, PETER USTINOV AND COLIN
GORDON.

and while my parents were talking about this and that, I used to stare and stare . . .

WICKED FAIRY. Who was it ?

DESMOND. The first of the Rinders. My mother's a Sparrow, you see. He was the Private Secretary to Lord Burghley's Personal Choirmaster, and died of a cholic condition in the late spring of 1616 . . .

WICKED FAIRY. Colonel, will you come on to the stage please.

DESMOND. Wish me luck.

WESLEY. Oh no. I'll wish myself that.

DESMOND. That attitude, Wesley, won't get you anywhere.

(He goes into the wings.)

WICKED FAIRY *(calling into the orchestra pit)*. Orchestra ! The music of England's Golden Age !

(A pavane is started. AIMÉ *enters, right, back in uniform. He seems weary. The* WICKED FAIRY *disappears once more behind the curtains.)*

WESLEY. Ah, Aimé. We've been discussing the motivations.

AIMÉ. I failed. I knew I would.

WESLEY. But why in hell did you insist that she was married ?

AIMÉ. Does it not disgust you when men of our age throw our shadow over youth and blissful inexperience ? I am a lover, Wesley, not a corrupter.

WESLEY. Do you mean you were being unselfish ?

AIMÉ. It is a relief when selfishness and unselfishness come to the same thing. I do not enjoy seducing youth. I can no longer bear to see the hope in its eyes. The hope of permanency—of eternity. It dazzles me, and leads me to behave like a fool. I like laughing at others, not at myself.

IKONENKO. But who is Jeanette ?

AIMÉ. Jeanette ? My mistress in Paris.

WESLEY. The actress ?

AIMÉ. The actress. She is not beautiful, but she is sad, and I like sadness. She is also safe. We lost our illusions with our second kiss, and our third was more passionate than the first.

IKONENKO. Still, you made every effort to make love to the Beauty.

AIMÉ. I wonder if I did.

IKONENKO.   Your attitude was clear to the spectator.   Clear and reprehensible.

AIMÉ.   I am so armoured against disappointment that I never make every effort any more.   I am a man.   She is beautiful. You might call her my ideal—and yet, as I have no ideals, my very love was tempered with misgiving.   I saw Jeanette again with what was almost relief.

WESLEY.   Tell me, as man to man, what do you see in Jeanette ?

GOOD FAIRY (*entering*).   What does any man see in his conscience ?

IKONENKO (*to* AIMÉ).   I fail to understand, Frappot, how you can have chosen as a favourite period the epoch of pre-revolutionary France.

AIMÉ.   Why ?

IKONENKO.   The insincerities which led relentlessly to the revolution were already painfully in evidence.

AIMÉ (*lively*).   Insincerities ?   By God, they said what they thought in those days, and said it wittily.

IKONENKO.   Wit is unnecessary.

AIMÉ.   So is life.

IKONENKO.   No, my friend, you are wrong.   Life is necessary, for without life, the world would be unpopulated.

AIMÉ.   And a great relief.

IKONENKO.   That is an offensive remark.

GOOD FAIRY.   I quite agree.

IKONENKO.   Without population, there could be no working class.   That is in itself enough sufficient reason for population.

GOOD FAIRY.   And where does God take his place in your conception ?

WICKED FAIRY (*looking through the curtains*).   Stop canvassing ! Silence please.   The play begins, I hope this time with satisfactory results.

GOOD FAIRY.   That depends upon you.

(*The music stops.   The lights go down.   The curtain rises.   Dim corridors of castle.   DESMOND is discovered, bearded, and dressed in elaborate Elizabethan costume.*)

DESMOND.   The day speeds sullenly to its decline
And all's yet unachieved.   There lingers in the mind
A vision of such galling purity

That I must defile it quick, or call myself
No more, Desmonio.
Five grey eagles cackled at my birth
And the entrails of a wasp lay, by dint of magick,
At my moaning mother's feet, who, being brought to bed
Of a two-months' child, did presently faint,
And pine, and die, aweary of her sire's black reproaches,
Which, being the first sounds to play upon this Desmon's ear,
Did fill full his thoughts with hatred of all chastity.
Thus with the light of the lately-dwindled moon
Did I pit my passion against an Illyrian nun—
"My vows, my vows", she cried, but 'twas in vain—
A maidenhead well lost's a mistress' gain.

(*Trumpets. He exits. The* BEAUTY *enters, sleepwalking. She is
fair, lovely, and desperately Elizabethan.*)

IKONENKO.   This is more like the Beauty.
AIMÉ.   It is ridiculous.   This one had no temperament.   I can
see it already.
IKONENKO.   Who is this Illyrian nun ?
WESLEY.   Don't ask me.   I know he was in Yugoslavia just
after the liberation.

(*The* BEAUTY *crosses the stage, sleepwalking, and exits.* DESMOND
enters from the opposite side of the stage.)

DESMOND.   The Fates, those horrid beldams
Who do play at tennis with our fortunes,
Do just now score a point in their portentous game.
For here's Aurora, betrothed to chastity,
But robbed of her entire kin by agencie
Of poison in the sacramental wine.
I'll to her while her heart's enfeebled by her grief.
For when a man is bent on sin
His conscience does fly out, his lewdness in !

(*Exit. Trumpets. The* BEAUTY *comes on from the opposite side
from which* DESMOND *has exitted.*)

BEAUTY.   Ah, could I but wile away the restless hours
Enshrouded in oblivion, then could the mind
Wander as a cloud, unanchored, midst th' uncharted stars,

And seek a refuge beyond imagination's reach.
Logic I abhor, and this woman's shape
A prison is. These hands, ten twigs, but petal-soft,
These arms, roads that lead into the air
From this all-too-solid dish of garnished bones
That men lust after. These breasts, that never will give suck,
But are as waterfalls dried up i' the heat
Of the desert sun, or as the eyes of one
With no more tears to weep. This face,
This outline of perfection, this sketch of beauty,
This mirror which, held up, reflects the nothingness within.
This belly this empty cell, this resting place
Of the unborn, forever uninhabited, an echoing vault,
My goldless treasury, my starless night.
These legs, these slender columns which bind me to the earth,
These restless travellers whose path runs wild
From the nowhere of birth to the nowhere of death
Through the nowhere in between. I have grown
Weary of breathing. Patience, enfold me then,
And death, be kind.
    DESMOND (*entering*). Death be kind,
But life be kinder first.
    BEAUTY. What's he that enters ? Art thou a ghost ?
    DESMOND. Nay, Aurora, but a geographie of rivers red
Which break their banks and rush for thee
In one cascading tide. Musick, ho !

              (*Music.*)

    BEAUTY. How dulcet is the virginall.
    DESMOND. And dulcet thou, of all most **virginall.**
    BEAUTY. Art thou a man ? For if thou art
Get thee to some more frolicksome abode
And do thy wenching there.
    DESMOND. I shall stay here, and we will **sink**
Our frantick hearts in a sweet sleep.

          (*He seizes her.*)

    BEAUTY (*Livid, throwing him away.*). Thou toad-spawn, thine
                own second worser self,
Thou yellow-painted bauble, thou toy, thou gadfly,

Thou wasp without a sting, thou twilight of a man,
Thou yolkless egg, thou image of decrepitude,
I'll none of thee. Go sing thy amorous odes to statues,
Get with child a tree-stump. Marry a broomstick. Away.

DESMOND. Say you so ? Then if I have thee not
Let no man have thee !

(*He draws a knife. The* WICKED FAIRY *enters as a Clown. The* GOOD FAIRY *rises precipitately.*)

GOOD FAIRY. He's done it again ! (*She rushes out.*)

WICKED FAIRY. Hold sirrah ! 'Tis of no avail to stab a monument.

DESMOND. A monument, say you ?

WICKED FAIRY. Ay, marry, a monument, upon which
        mournful pigeons sit,
And spill their droppings, which do go for tears.

BEAUTY. Oh, foolish fool.

WICKED FAIRY. How should I not be foolish, being a fool, for were I not a fool, I would be wise, the less like thee, for thou, good lady, art in no wise wise, and no wise foolish, and not foolish wise, and no wit either, for to be without wit is to be neither, therefore thou'rt in no wit wise and in no wise witty, and fall'st on thy bum 'twixt Grandam Nature's twin stools.

BEAUTY. I am in no humour for mirth, boy.

WICKED FAIRY (*imitating her*). I am in no humour for mirth, wench.

WESLEY. This must have amused the audiences of the time.

BEAUTY. I weep.

WICKED FAIRY. Nay, nay, an' thou weeps't, thou art no monument. Thou art a fountain, lady. I shall go abroad, and weep myself, and say, " My lady is the breathing stuff of sprats, the nourishment of frogs, the comforter of dogs, for they do cock their legs at her as I do cock my snook." (*He pulls a long nose.*)

BEAUTY. My tears do turn to tears of laughter,
And I do hate thee for it.

DESMOND (*aside*). This boy doth serve my purpose well.

WICKED FAIRY. Hate me, madam, if it help thee know thyself, for I am much-hated Tom-a-Green, or Tickle-Rib, or Itch-Side, or Cackle-Face, or Grin-Jowl, or Chuckle-Head, or Wit-Nit, and I have as many names as I have faces, an' if there's one of me you hate, there's ten more left to love.

BEAUTY. Thou sayest true, boy, and I do love thee well.

WICKED FAIRY. Nay, lavish not thy love on me. There is another, worthier far, who is so fine and great a one, he does not walk but in a pavan, does not run but in a corranto, and does not stand still but in a gracious and tempestuous attitude.

BEAUTY. Why tempestuous, boy?

WICKED FAIRY. It is the longest word I know.

BEAUTY. Who is this suitor, boy?

WICKED FAIRY. His name, Desmonio.

BEAUTY. Desmonio. It is a name which doth
Make music of a moan. I'll to him straight.

DESMOND. But straighter he to thee.

BEAUTY. Desmonio.

DESMOND. How is my name lullabied upon that tongue,
And bathed in breath as sweet as rose's scent.
The name is not enough. The man must follow.

BEAUTY (*seeing him*). Art thou Desmonio, then?

DESMOND. The same.

BEAUTY. How have I wronged thee! Thy eagerness deceived.

(DESMOND *holds* BEAUTY *in his arms.*)

DESMOND. The veil of sorrow's lifted, all's well, Aurora.
Come into the halter of my arms, and shake not off
Thy new-found shackles till th' impudent sun
Does peep through his drapery of morning clouds
To tease young lovers out of sleep. Nay, speak not,
For silence is the language that we lovers speak.

BEAUTY. And yet I must. O sweet Desmonio, now
All nature is abuzz with living.
Summer and spring do lie within my heart
And play at paramours. I am invaded
With a love which knows no satisfaction,
For it would stretch to the furthest frontiers o' the senses
Like an all-consuming tide, and o'er-reaching itself at last,
Fall into a slumber as sweet
As is the word serenity.

DESMOND. Let's to't then.

(*The* GOOD FAIRY *enters as a Ghost.*)

BEAUTY (*shrieks*). It is my mother! All's ill wi' me!

DESMOND (*releasing her*).   Th' Illyrian nun !

WICKED FAIRY (*transcendentally angry*).   **Oh,** no !   Curtain !
Bring it down !   Give me time to think !

(THE CURTAIN-WITHIN-A-CURTAIN AND THE MAIN CURTAIN BOTH
FALL.)

ACT III

A few minutes later. WESLEY *and the* TWO FAIRIES *are absent.*
DESMOND *is there, back in uniform.   There has evidently been a
pause for sombre meditation.*

DESMOND.   I say, was I awfully embarrassing ?   I mean, did I
let a lot of cats out of the proverbial bag ?
AIMÉ.   Quite enough.   Do you write poetry ?
DESMOND (*embarrassed*).   Oh, that.   Just for fun.   Not
seriously.
AIMÉ.   Like so many English, you are permanently
embarrassed.
DESMOND.   There's so damned much to be embarrassed about.
IKONENKO.   Have you ever published a poem ?
DESMOND (*laughs softly*).   Yes, I have.   Twice.   One in the
Observer, the other time in *Country Life*.   I took a woman's name
to write both, thought they'd have a better chance.   I was right.
IKONENKO (*shocked*).   A woman's name !
DESMOND.   It doesn't do to have a Colonel writing about trees
and flowers, not in England—not on the active list.
IKONENKO.   Then you should not have written them at all.
AIMÉ.   Don't be ridiculous.   Desmond, you amaze me.   I
have often watched you, and I think I know you a little better
now.   God forbid, you will say.   You don't really want to be
known.
DESMOND (*embarrassed*).   I don't mind.
AIMÉ.   You are like so many of those strange and secret
English, with a genius for reflection.
IKONENKO.   Reflection ?   I fail to understand.   How can one
have a genius for such a passive quality ?
AIMÉ.   The English gaze at their countryside through a swirl of
pipe-smoke, through the sights of a huntsman's gun, from under
wet umbrellas, and they link all generations in their mind.
History is a reality, for the gigantic oaks are living witnesses of it.
The cliffs were already there to echo the trumpets of long-for-
gotten battles, while the mansions are but sleeping quarters for the

dead. The supernatural holds no surprises for them in the sacred preserves in which they wander with such unspoken relish. Only the present, the realistic commonplace, shocks them, and they are driven to embarrassed silence by the events of every day. That is the reason why you, Ikonenko, are so profoundly shocking to them.

IKONENKO. I fail to see why I should be profoundly shocking.

DESMOND. That's your charm, old man.

IKONENKO. On the contrary, you have made certain statements which I suspect to be of a highly scandalous nature.

DESMOND. Such as ?

IKONENKO. Who is this Illyrian nun ?

DESMOND (*puffing at his pipe. Grave*). Oh, nothing. I just behaved rather disgracefully to a Yugoslav girl when I was there.

IKONENKO. A nun ?

DESMOND. No, no. Just a girl. A young girl. I let her down. It was a caddish thing to do. Did I refer to her as a nun ?

IKONENKO. Yes.

DESMOND. Well, it just shows what the conscience will do to force its way into the imagination.

AIMÉ. The romantic imagination.

DESMOND. Oh, for heaven's sake, leave romance to Wesley.

AIMÉ. I wonder what we shall see ?

DESMOND. American Civil War, I wouldn't be surprised.

IKONENKO. Wall Street.

AIMÉ. That's probably more like it. I mistrust people who boast of their romanticism.

WICKED FAIRY (*through the curtains*). Orchestra ! Cacophony, please.

(*He disappears. The orchestra plays a highly sentimental blues.*)

AIMÉ. That sounds promising.

DESMOND. It seems Donovan's going to stay up there.

IKONENKO. She has understood the full measure of Carabosse's duplicity.

DESMOND. Here we go . . .

(*The curtain rises on the outline of a honky-tonk bar. The BEAUTY is sitting at the bar, an unmistakable street-walker, puffing at a long cigarette-holder. She gazes out with the idealized melancholy of her profession.*)

DESMOND.   Good gracious !

IKONENKO (*rising*).   This is an outrage !

AIMÉ.   Sit down, sit down.   Wait for the hero of fiction.   Here he comes . . .

(WESLEY *enters, dressed as a clergyman.*)

DESMOND.   I say, he told me his greatest ambition was to lead the Charge of the Light Brigade.

AIMÉ.   You took us by surprise, Desmond.   You must allow him the same privilege.

(WESLEY *sits at the single table, and lights a cigarette.*)

IKONENKO.   What sort of uniform is he wearing ?

AIMÉ.   He is a priest.

IKONENKO.   A counter-revolutionary !

WESLEY.   Cigarette ? (*Silence.*)   Cigarette ?

BEAUTY.   Are you talking to me ?

WESLEY.   Yeah, I guess I was.

BEAUTY.   If you want me, I'll give you a price.   I don't go for opening gambits.

WESLEY (*with a self-righteous smile*).   I don't . . . em . . . want you.   I was offering you a cigarette.

BEAUTY (*incredulous*).   For free ?

WESLEY.   Sure.

BEAUTY (*staggered*).   Hey, what kind of a fellow are you ?

WESLEY.   Can't you see ?

BEAUTY.   Yeah, I can see.   I got eyes.   Listen, you oughta be in church.   This is no place for you.

WESLEY.   You're wrong, kid.   This is for me, and it's you ought to be right there in church.

BEAUTY.   Yeah ?   You talk like my father.

WESLEY.   Where is your father ?

BEAUTY.   Dead.   Cold.   Flat.

WESLEY.   I'm sorry.

BEAUTY.   Me, I'm glad.

(*Pause.*)

WESLEY.   What's your name, child ?

BEAUTY.   Hey, where d'you get that " child " from ?

WESLEY.   We are all——

BEAUTY. I know. God's kids. I got loaded with that boloney at Sunday School.

WESLEY (*laughing*). We're going to have quite a time putting you right, my dear.

BEAUTY. If you want to keep that purty smile on your kisser, you just won't try, that's all.

WESLEY. You haven't told me your name.

BEAUTY. What's it to you?

WESLEY. I'm Father Brietenspiegel. They call me the Fighting Father.

BEAUTY (*impressed*). Hey, are you Fighting Father Brietenspiegel? *The* Fighting Father Breitenspiegel?

WESLEY. Sure. The guy that started Girls' Town. Now will you tell me your name?

BEAUTY. Aurora-Mae Duckworth.

WESLEY. Aurora-Mae. Kinda cute name.

BEAUTY. They call me Rory.

WESLEY. Who's they?

BEAUTY. Guys.

WESLEY. Which guys?

BEAUTY. How do I know? I only see them once, if that.

(*The wail of a train's siren is heard.*)

WESLEY. What's that?

BEAUTY. The Cincinnatti Chieftain, bringing them into town.

WESLEY. Bringing who into town?

BEAUTY (*with a shrug*). Customers.

WESLEY. Listen, Rory, I want you to know something.

BEAUTY. Something I don't know?

WESLEY. Sure. The world's not like you think it is.

BEAUTY. The world's tough like last week's steak.

WESLEY. Sure it's tough, but it's kinda great and beautiful, too.

BEAUTY. Brother, that's not my world. Keep it. You're welcome to it.

WESLEY. You, too, Rory, you're welcome to it.

BEAUTY. Thanks all the same, but I'm a working girl.

WESLEY. I want to take you away from here, Rory, but bad.

BEAUTY. Why don't you shut up?

WESLEY. Ever seen the sun rise over the Alleghanies, Rory? It comes up like a great big lantern in the sky, and seems to say, "Get up, get up" to all God's creatures. "I'm back again,

folks," it says, " I've been keeping guys warm right the other side
of the great wide world, but I've kept my promise to you, and
now I'm right back here with you till my old pal the moon comes
back to-night." And you'd kneel there, Rory, filling your billy-
can by the brook, and say to it, "Thanks, sun, it's sure good to
see you back. You're a pal." And the old sun'ud say, " Don't
thank me, Rory, I'm just doing my duty, drawing my lantern
from the mountains in the morning, and dipping it into the ocean
at night. I'm doing my duty, Rory—are you ? " And you'd
think, and smile up at the old boy up there, and say, " Sure, Mr.
Sun, I've left the city lights way back of me "—and then you'd
add, " Sorry, feller, I'll be seeing you. It's my turn to build the
bonfire for breakfast at Girls' Town." " What's cookin' kids ? "
he'll call, " Waffles with maple syrup, ham, cornflakes, and real
good coffee." Then, if it rains, Rory, you'll know it's just the
poor old fellow's mouth watering.

AIMÉ.   I have an irresistible desire to brush my teeth.

BEAUTY (*visibly moved*).   I'm sorry, Father—you're too late.

(*The door opens, and the* WICKED FAIRY *enters dressed as a gangster.
His face is practically concealed in the upturned collar of his
overcoat, beneath which can be seen the striped trousers of a
convict.*)

BEAUTY.   Hey.   Just go on talking to me, that's all.

WESLEY.   What's wrong ?

BEAUTY.   Please.   Pretend to know me.

WESLEY.   Who is that guy, Rory ?

WICKED FAIRY.   Don't I get any service round here ?

BEAUTY (*urgent*).   Don't answer.

WICKED FAIRY.   Anybody got ears ?

WESLEY.   Why yes, I have.

WICKED FAIRY (*swinging round*).   Then keep them shut, if you
know what's good. (*Smirking.*) Hiya, Rory. You didn't figure
you'd see me again so soon, huh ?

BEAUTY.   What are you doing here ?   You got a ninety-nine-
year stretch.

WICKED FAIRY.   I came out on parole, honey, just to see
you.

WESLEY.   Hey, didn't I see your face in the newspaper ?

WICKED FAIRY (*sinister, grinning*).   Sure.   I take good
pictures, huh ?   Oughta be in Hollywood, playing heavies.

WESLEY. You're Tony Carabosse. You didn't come out on parole. You broke jail.

WICKED FAIRY. O.K., wise guy. So I granted myself parole. What's the difference ?

WESLEY. Why, that's illegal !

WICKED FAIRY (*to* BEAUTY). Hey, what kind of brainy guys are you going with these days, sugar ?

BEAUTY. What do you want, Tony ?

WICKED FAIRY. I want to settle a little argument we never finished, baby. Remember the time the cops came, and you kept going to the window, said you felt hot ? Sure you felt hot, you dirty double-crossing she-dog. Yeah.

BEAUTY (*nervous, not without reason*). Say what you have to, and beat it.

WICKED FAIRY. What I've got on my mind don't explain itself with words.

BEAUTY (*still more nervous*). What do you mean ?

WICKED FAIRY. I'm so big, sweetheart, I've got a friend to do my arguing for me. (*He draws a gun.*)

WESLEY. Put that gun away.

WICKED FAIRY. Button your lip.

WESLEY. Have you a licence for that firearm ?

WICKED FAIRY. Sure, bishop, I even got a diploma.

BEAUTY. You wouldn't dare shoot me !

WICKED FAIRY. No ?

WESLEY. You'd be guilty of first-degree murder.

WICKED FAIRY. You're wrong, saint, I got me a good lawyer. I never get more than second degree.

WESLEY. You will this time.

WICKED FAIRY. How come ?

WESLEY. I'll be right there in the courtroom.

WICKED FAIRY. You'll be a patch of grass, brother. I'll pump you both with lead. A guy can't die twice, and if I go, you're coming right along with me.

(*Pause. The* WICKED FAIRY *sits down.*)

Yeah, funny thing. I'm in a generous mood. I'll let the both of you kneel down and say your prayers.

WESLEY. It's not too late for salvation, Tony. Kneel down with us and be saved.

WICKED FAIRY. Are you kidding ? I'll give you one more

chance, sugar, and then it's curtains. I figure I've gotten to that time in a guy's life when he kinda wants something different, something solid. I'm going straight, kid.

WESLEY (*ecstatic, juggling with haloes*). You're going straight?

WICKED FAIRY. Sure, after I've bumped you off, I'm going straight. Going to run a gambling ship off the coast of Mexico. Strictly on the level. I've got dough. Plenty dough. A guy don't live for ever.

WESLEY. He may inherit the life everlasting, even at this late stage.

WICKED FAIRY. Don't give me that!

BEAUTY. Don't give us that, will you?

WICKED FAIRY. Listen, babe, I want a kid. A kid can take over the gambling ship when I'm cold.

BEAUTY (*livid*). Are you suggesting marriage?

WICKED FAIRY. Don't say it that way, it don't sound so good.

BEAUTY. Listen, louse, I go with guys, but I don't marry them. That's not me. I'm not made that way. That's not the way I tick. I'm one of the little people, that like little, simple things. I don't get big ideas, the way you do. I'm little, and I like little guys, guys that go to the ball-game Sundays and stand right there and shout and put their souls into their shouting, and love and cry and live and die down here by the railroad track. I don't want big ideas, Tony Carabosse, on account of they eat you up, like fire, from the inside. All that was once laughter and sadness gets like it was strictly business, and you get cold and hard and treat the human soul like it was real estate. It's guys like you that drive honest school-kids to crime and slaughter and all those other big things I only heard talk about, and it's guys like you try to smash the little things, and the beautiful deep things, and the U.S. Constitution. They ought to brand you right there on the forehead, where all the little guys can see, "This is the enemy," in letters of flaming red.

IKONENKO. Has she refused?

BEAUTY (*vastly superior*). And there's something else. Thomas Jefferson once said——

WICKED FAIRY (*breathing*). O.K., sister. You asked for this.

(*He is about to shoot, when* WESLEY *expertly knocks the gun out of his hand, and confiscates it.*)

Why you——

WESLEY. Stay where you are.

WICKED FAIRY (*quavering*). Don't do it. Don't shoot me. I'll give you a partnership in the gambling hell, reverend. Fifty grand down, and I'll pay your taxes.

WESLEY. Why, you poor misguided child. I'm going to call the District Attorney, but first——

WICKED FAIRY. They got dames in Mexico. Swell dames.

WESLEY (*louder*). But first——

WICKED FAIRY. And dough.

WESLEY (*louder still*). But first——

WICKED FAIRY. Liquor.

WESLEY (*even louder*). But first——

WICKED FAIRY. Automobiles . . .

WESLEY (*shouting*). But first, I'm going to teach you a little Scripture lesson.

WICKED FAIRY (*falling to his knees*). Oh no, not that!

WESLEY. Sure. (*He places one hand pontifically on the* WICKED FAIRY'S *head, while with the other he holds the gun to his temple.*) Samson smote the Philistine host with the jawbone of an ass. "And he found a new jawbone of an ass, and put forth his hand, and took it, and slew a thousand men therewith." I'm not that ambitious. I take them on one at a time.

(*He throws down the revolver. After a moment of indecision, the* WICKED FAIRY *makes a dive for it.* WESLEY *is too quick for him, seizes him, lifts him into the air, and sends him reeling into the corner with a fierce uppercut. The orchestra helps the illusion. The* BEAUTY *encourages* WESLEY, *who rushes at the* WICKED FAIRY. *The* WICKED FAIRY *places his feet on* WESLEY'S *stomach and sends him tottering back. The* WICKED FAIRY, *with a superhuman effort, wrenches the top section off the juke box, and staggers towards* WESLEY *with it.* WESLEY *takes the juke box away from him easily with one hand, discards it, and then proceeds to deal the* WICKED FAIRY *some brutal, but apparently ineffectual blows, for the* WICKED FAIRY *always comes back for more. At length twelve tremendous uppercuts, accompanied by the orchestral drums, send the* WICKED FAIRY *uneasily to the ground. One writhe, and all is stillness.* WESLEY *smoothes his hair with his hand. The* BEAUTY *awaits his embrace.*)

BEAUTY. O.K., feller, you win. When do we leave?

WESLEY. Leave?

BEAUTY. For Girls' Town. I never felt more religious in my life.

WESLEY. Then . . . you will come ?

BEAUTY. You're a funny guy.

WESLEY. Why ?

BEAUTY. You've been fightin' over me, haven't you ?

WESLEY. In a way . . .

BEAUTY (*her arms open*). Then why don't you take me, you dope ?

WESLEY. I wasn't fighting just for you, Rory, but for the forces of light and freedom all over the world.

BEAUTY (*seductive*). That's as maybe, but it's me you want.

WESLEY. Don't talk that way. That's horrible . . . (*A sudden realization.*) That's temptation !

BEAUTY (*very much in love*). It's just old man nature knocking at our door.

WESLEY (*powerful*). I have come to save you from the abyss, not to be dragged down myself !

BEAUTY (*sadly*). You got me wrong, butch.

WESLEY. My name is Wesley.

BEAUTY. I never lived like this. This is my first day's work.

WESLEY. Then you mean—— ?

BEAUTY. Yeah. I was in love with Tony, sure. He was going to be my man—and then . . . something inside me snapped, I guess.

WESLEY (*urgent*). You called the police ?

BEAUTY. Yeah. I sent my man to the big house. He was going to be my first. After that, well, life was hard . . . I'd read books. I guess I took to it easy. Cut my dresses short. Got hold of eyeblack, lipred. Used my hips. I was all ready for the first guy to come along. And that guy had to be you !

WESLEY (*foolishly radiant*). Then I have saved you ! Saved you from blemish !

BEAUTY. That's the way it looks.

WESLEY (*earnest*). What do you want out of life, Aurora-Mae ?

BEAUTY (*much too fierce*). I want a guy I can *respect* !

WESLEY (*jaw rippling. Exaggerately manly*). I'm crazy about you, Rory, you must know that. I want you to marry me.

BEAUTY. But—— ?

WESLEY. I know what you're thinking. Listen, my dear . . . my darling—they only call me " Father." I'm an Episcopalian.

BEAUTY. Whoopee ! Hold me tight. Tighter. (*Her eyes shut in ecstasy.*) My holy dreamboat ! My Noah's ark !

(*They are about to kiss when the* GOOD FAIRY *enters, bespectacled and grim.*)

GOOD FAIRY. So there you are, Wesley Breitenspiegel.
BEAUTY. Who's this ?
WESLEY (*agonized*). Why do you follow me around ?
BEAUTY (*ready for disenchantment*). Is she your girl ?
WESLEY. No.
BEAUTY. Your wife ?
WESLEY. No. My psychiatrist.
GOOD FAIRY. Now come away from that girl, Wesley, and just relax completely.

(WESLEY *breaks away obediently, and sits down on the chair which the* GOOD FAIRY *provides.*)

BEAUTY. What's wrong with him ? Is it a war wound ?
GOOD FAIRY. He mustn't have excitement of any sort. Wesley, make your mind a complete blank. My dear girl, don't pursue this matter further. Take my advice.
BEAUTY (*fiercely*). But he loves me ! He wants to marry me !
GOOD FAIRY. Illusion, my dear. Just a superimposition of the mother image onto you. *Very* unfortunate. He's always going round trying to marry girls. It's part of the illness.
BEAUTY. But . . . but Girls' Town . . . ?
GOOD FAIRY. Exactly, my dear.

(*The* WICKED FAIRY *staggers to his feet. He seizes the revolver.*)

WICKED FAIRY. O.K., wise guys . . . (*He sees the horror-struck* BEAUTY, *the grimly functional* GOOD FAIRY, *and the glazed-eyed* WESLEY, *and says, resignedly—*) Oh, what's the use. Curtain. Bring it down.

(*The curtain falls.*)

AIMÉ. Well, there's our great romantic, our Don Quixote who has to ask a policeman the way to the windmills.
IKONENKO. He demonstrated very clearly the hysterical undertones of contemporary Pluto-Fascist society.
DESMOND. No, I can't allow that, old man. He just showed evidence of a deeply moral upbringing at a school which was undoubtedly a sight too good.

IKONENKO. Too good ? A school cannot be good or bad, it can only be accurate or inaccurate.

DESMOND. Oh, nonsense, old fellow. I went to a school which is generally considered the best there is. Well, it was far too good to produce really useful citizens.

AIMÉ. How about you ?

DESMOND. I flatter myself that my one saving grace is that I was such a bad pupil. But thanks for the compliment.

(*The* WICKED FAIRY *looks through the curtains.*)

WICKED FAIRY (*depressed*). Next please. Colonel Ikonenko.

IKONENKO. I do not wish to take part in the experiment.

AIMÉ. What ?

WICKED FAIRY. Don't you love the girl ?

IKONENKO. What is the meaning of such a word ? Is it a realistic approach to life to say that you are at any time in love ?

DESMOND. Good gracious me. Realism can be carried too far, you know.

IKONENKO. No. People who have never seen a bath do not want a bath. That is realistic. Knowledge breeds desire, and desire breeds hatred.

WICKED FAIRY (*sly*). Yes, but you have seen the girl. You know her.

IKONENKO. Unfortunately.

WICKED FAIRY. Those flaxen curls, that freckled face, those strong arms and legs, that healthy, child-bearing body. Can you resist it ?

IKONENKO (*after a pause. Rises*). I shall go just to see her again. For no other reason.

WICKED FAIRY. Which period do you wish to see her in ?

IKONENKO. A period in which they had the rounded epaulettes with golden tassels on them.

WICKED FAIRY (*smiling*). Orchestra. Valse Pathetique.

(*The orchestra begins to play a sentimental waltz.* IKONENKO *and the* WICKED FAIRY *go.*)

DESMOND. What an uncouth fellow.

AIMÉ. I wonder. I begin to see a little of his point of view.

DESMOND. Blowed if I do.

ACT III (*from left to right*) PETER USTINOV, MOIRA LISTER AND THEODORE BIKEL.

AIMÉ. Can we men really be in love with something so fragile, so unexplained, as an ideal ? Didn't we go up there to show off to each other, because we've heard the girl is beautiful ?

DESMOND. I thought she was beautiful, myself.

(WESLEY *enters, back in uniform.*)

Bad luck, Galahad.

WESLEY. I want to go back, out of this dream-world.

AIMÉ. Why ?

WESLEY. She's a great kid. A really swell kid. But I'm all tied up in knots.

AIMÉ. What knots ?

WESLEY. I just want to go back and talk to Doctor Polgeister. (*With a wan smile.*) That's the worst of being a romantic.

(DESMOND *and* AIMÉ *exchange looks. The lights dim. The curtains part to reveal a Chekhovian garden. Croquet hoops on the ground. The* BEAUTY, *dressed in* 1900 *costume, and stouter than before, is idly playing croquet.* IKONENKO *enters. He wears a dark green uniform with epaulettes ; he sits down on a garden swing, and begins knitting.*)

IKONENKO. So it is summer once again . . . who would have thought it . . .

BEAUTY. Summer seems to pass like a single hour when one is playing croquet . . . Anatol Lvovitch will be thirty-eight next birthday . . .

(*Pause.*)

IKONENKO. Excuse me, I have not been listening to what you have been saying . . .

BEAUTY. It was nothing . . .

IKONENKO. It was something . . . it was something . . . "Golden words tumble from your lips like a waterfall lit by the midnight sun " . . . that was Pushkin, I believe . . . great man, Pushkin. Greatest poet Russia ever had . . .

BEAUTY. I don't read . . .

IKONENKO. None of us read. You play croquet . . . I knit . . . I am knitting a pair of mittens for Kolya, the medical orderly . . . why do we do it ?

BEAUTY. Are we in love ?

IKONENKO. In love ?

BEAUTY. With life ? It is so important not to give up hope. (*She hits the croquet ball with her mallet.*) There, I have scored a splendid point, and there was nobody here to see it.

(*Pause. A shot rings out.*)

What was that ?

IKONENKO. A woodman felling a birch tree . . .

BEAUTY. It sounded to me like——

IKONENKO. It was raining in Kharkov last Friday. I know, because Grischa left his umbrella at the barracks.

BEAUTY. Ever since Papa died, I have never carried an umbrella. There were so many at the funeral . . .

IKONENKO. Was it raining ?

BEAUTY. No . . .

(*Pause.*)

IKONENKO. Now I have dropped a stitch, and must undo it all.

BEAUTY. I was so looking forward to yesterday.

IKONENKO. Sadovsky's dance ?

BEAUTY. Yes . . . but now that it is over, I cannot look forward to it any more . . .

IKONENKO. I did not go . . .

BEAUTY. Nor did I . . .

IKONENKO. I stayed here . . . in the drawing room . . . mending the General's watch . . .

BEAUTY. I was here too . . . in the dining-room . . . thinking . . .

IKONENKO. We were in the house alone . . .

BEAUTY. Yes . . .

IKONENKO. And I never knew . . .

(*The* WICKED FAIRY *enters, dressed in eccentric summer clothes, and with a long white beard.*)

WICKED FAIRY. Boo ! Do I interrupt an idyll ? Are the love-birds ruthlessly pecking one another ? Have I chanced upon a courtship in the aviary ?

BEAUTY. Uncle ! Dear, darling Uncle !

WICKED FAIRY. What ? Is my starling playing croquet, then ? Ah, but only until evening, I'll warrant ? Eh ? Then, when the moon emerges from her starry retreat . . . ? Eh ? Eh ? Do I make myself clear ?

IKONENKO. I must leave for Moscow to-night.

WICKED FAIRY. Eh ? Eh ?

BEAUTY. To-night ?

IKONENKO. They have given me a regiment in Kazakstan.

WICKED FAIRY. What a disgrace ! How you have upset me ! There is no telling what the authorities will do. Only yesterday I heard from Sadovsky, the old rascal, that Ignaty Ivanovitch Bulkin, the Associate Assessor of an intermediary grade, in a temporary capacity from the Rural Board, a dear but foolish man, kind but despicable, as you might say, if . . . so . . . inclined . . . a man, mark you, who never travels by train because the noise of the engine frightens him, he believes the devil to be sitting inside it, boiling water for his tea, well—where was I ? I'm getting old.

BEAUTY. Dear, dear Uncle.

WICKED FAIRY. Ah, yes—this man has been made Inspector-General of the local railway, if you please ! If it were true, it would be absolutely scandalous. Fortunately Sadovsky is as unreliable as I am, may God and his saints forgive me, and there is no possibility of it being true. All the same, it has excited me somewhat. I really must sit down. (*He sits. Then pretends to shoot into the air with an imaginary gun.*) Piff ! Paff ! Pouff ! (*He raises his imaginary rifle to shoot again when another shot rings out, off stage.*) I enjoy shooting seagulls, but it is less cruel without a gun.

BEAUTY. There is that noise again . . . there cannot be many birch trees left . . . my poor, lovely birch trees . . .

WICKED FAIRY. That's no birch tree. It is Uncle Mischa trying to shoot himself. It really is degrading how he fails at everything he puts his hand to. So bad for the family's name. While, as an ex-officer, his inability to shoot straight is a direct reflection on His Imperial Majesty's Army. But there, I must not excite myself. If one took everything to heart, where would one be . . . where would one be . . . why, just exactly where one is . . .

BEAUTY. Dear, darling Uncle. Why does Uncle Mischa do it ?

WICKED FAIRY. He is in love . . .

BEAUTY. With life . . . like me ?

WICKED FAIRY. He is in love with . . . a certain party . . . a pretty little starling who passes her youth in playing croquet. But there, I talk too much, as always . . .

BEAUTY.   In five or six hundred years . . . perhaps then I will be happy . . .

(*Pause. Suddenly the* WICKED FAIRY *gets up, furious, tears off his wig, and pushes his false beard up onto his forehead.*)

WICKED FAIRY (*to* IKONENKO; *out of character*).   Damn it, you're just not trying !
IKONENKO.   Why should I try ?   Haven't I seen what happened to the others ?
WICKED FAIRY.   I give you one last chance.   Will you seduce her or not ?
IKONENKO.   No !

(*The* GOOD FAIRY *enters, much stouter than before, with a black wig and horrible bun. She is dressed from head to foot in black.*)

GOOD FAIRY.   D'you mean to say I've got dressed for nothing ?
IKONENKO.   Aha !   You are my wife.   I knew you would come if I tried to seduce her.   What's the use ?   I'd rather sit quietly knitting in my Beauty's company than invoke you.

(*The* BEAUTY, *who has been idling with the croquet mallet, suddenly looks up, and sees her beloved Uncle without his hair, and with his beard apparently growing out of the top of his head. She screams, pointing at him, and swoons.*)

GOOD FAIRY (*upset—to* WICKED FAIRY).   Now look what you've done !   (*She runs over to comfort the* BEAUTY.)
WICKED FAIRY (*furious*).   The interlude is over !   Curtain once again !   For the last time !

(*The curtain falls.*)

AIMÉ.   Well, that's that.
WESLEY.   What in hell's the matter with that guy ?
DESMOND.   Thoroughly cynical, if you ask me.
AIMÉ.   No, I don't agree.   I call him uncomfortably intelligent.
WESLEY.   I don't feel I can work with any of you again after this.
DESMOND.   I want to get back, and double quick.   I'll have a word about it with Donovan.   Funny, but I don't entirely trust the other fellow.

(*The* GOOD FAIRY *enters,* R.   *She is in her A.T.S. uniform again.*)

GOOD FAIRY.   Well, have you decided ? Do you want to stay ?
CHORUS.   No.
GOOD FAIRY.   You realize you will never defile the Beauty
while I prevent you.
AIMÉ.   But you still want us to reach for the unattainable.
You want us to stay.
GOOD FAIRY.   How do you know what I want ?
AIMÉ.   Carabosse also realizes that the Beauty is incor-
ruptible, so he——
WICKED FAIRY (*looking through the curtains*).   What does he
want you to do ?
AIMÉ.   Ah, there you are—you wish us to return to the wilder-
ness of normal life, where we can deceive our wives at your
pleasure.

(*The* WICKED FAIRY *and the* GOOD FAIRY *exchange glances.*)

GOOD FAIRY.   Stay—with perfection.
AIMÉ.   Why do you make perfection sound so desirable ?
WICKED FAIRY.   Well, isn't it ?
AIMÉ.   Is it ?
GOOD FAIRY.   It's . . . it's very peaceful . . .
AIMÉ.   Exactly.   It's very boring.
WICKED FAIRY (*lively*).   Very well, you know-all.   Yes, I want
you to return.   But I'll be fair to Donovan.   If you sin, you must
sin with conviction.   I'm sick of empty victories.   So if you'll
return to your seats, I'll show you what you may expect to return
to.

(IKONENKO *enters, back in uniform.*)

DESMOND.   What are you driving at, sir ? Nothing's happened
in our absence, has it ?
WICKED FAIRY.   Oh, yes . . .
WESLEY.   Well, tell us.   There's not another war, is there ?
WICKED FAIRY.   Not yet.
IKONENKO.   Has a superior arrived from Moscow, and I was not
there to receive him ?
WICKED FAIRY.   You're getting warmer.

AIMÉ.   Have we all got visitors ?

WICKED FAIRY.   Yes.

DESMOND.   Well, show us, for heaven's sake. Stop insinuating.

WICKED FAIRY.   Are you ready ? Orchestra. (*He squats and talks among the palms, sotto voce.*)

(*The orchestra begins Chopin's Funeral March.   The lights dim.*)

DESMOND.   Good gracious, someone's died.

GOOD FAIRY (*sad*).   Don't worry. It's only Carabosse's cynicism. The music is intended to be descriptive rather than elegaic.

(*The curtain rises slowly, and the* WICKED FAIRY *comes back among the* COLONELS.   *The scene is the set of Act* I. *Now* FOUR WOMEN *sit around in silence.   One is gaunt, wears a shapeless hat, and regimental jewellery.* DESMOND *recognizes her immediately.*)

DESMOND.   Mabel !

(*Another is terribly chic, wears a hat with vast feathers.*)

AIMÉ.   Thérèse !

(*Another is tweedily smart, wears glasses.*)

WESLEY.   Shirley !

(*Another is stout, and resembles the* GOOD FAIRY'S *last disguise. She holds a newly-born baby.*)

IKONENKO.   Olga !

GOOD FAIRY.   Yes, after two and a half years of negotiation, the four powers have reached agreement, and given your wives permission to join you.

DESMOND.   And we weren't there to meet them !

WICKED FAIRY.   Don't say you wanted to be there ?

DESMOND.   That doesn't enter into it, old man. It's *done*.

WESLEY.   Why don't they say anything ? They're not dead, are they ?

WICKED FAIRY.   No. (*Calls.*) Stop the music !

(The music stops.)

MABEL. We seem to have run out of conversation . . .
SHIRLEY. Yeah . . .

(The baby starts yelling fitfully.)

IKONENKO. What is that child doing here ?
WICKED FAIRY *(laughing)*. It's yours.
DESMOND. Don't be ridiculous, he's been away two and a half years.
WICKED FAIRY. Quite.
GOOD FAIRY. Oh, you cruel, cruel fairy.
IKONENKO. Am I to understand that I am not the father ?
DESMOND. I'm terribly sorry, old chum.
IKONENKO. Such events are only to be expected in difficult times.
WESLEY. Do you mean to sit there and tell me you don't mind ? Why, I'd divorce her, find the guy that's responsible and beat the living daylights óut of him.
DESMOND. I will not conceal the fact that I am profoundly shocked at your attitude, sir.
IKONENKO. Why should I—— ?

(Before he can finish his sentence, MABEL, who has been consulting a jewelled watch, says—)

MABEL. Do you realize we've been here for two hours ?
SHIRLEY. And no sign of the boys. Well, they can't say they didn't get the cables, because here they are, right on the table.
THERÈSE. What do you expect from men ?
SHIRLEY. I demand a certain degree of courtesy. After all, I'm a hard-working woman. I have to fly to Frankfurt to-morrow, Rome Friday and back here Sunday.
MABEL. You won't see much of Rome in two days.
SHIRLEY. I don't go there to see it, Mrs. Sparrow—I work. I'm the women's editress of a group of syndicated magazines, including *Wife*, a woman's magazine with a difference, *Urge*, which is a frank journal for children in the difficult age, and *Think*, a more mature publication dealing with the psychological aspects of marriage in general and matrimonial misfits in particular. I'm being advised in all this by Orlando Kisfaludy—

WESLEY.   The bastard.

SHIRLEY.   —one of the greatest alienists we have in the States.

WESLEY.   Oh God, she talks an awful lot.

SHIRLEY.   And then, of course——

THERÈSE.   I don't understand what there is left to talk about on the subject of marriage.

AIMÉ.   Bravo, Therèse.

SHIRLEY.   Oh, one hell of a lot.   I'm just inundated with material.   I've gotten very much more than I can use.

WESLEY.   That's always been your trouble, honey.   You use it all the same.

SHIRLEY (*shrewdly*).   Of course, I am helped by having a husband who is psychologically unstable.

WESLEY.   Hey !

THERÈSE.   Aren't they all ?

MABEL (*shocked*).   I trust not !

DESMOND.   Oh, shut up, Mabel dear.

SHIRLEY.   Well, in a way, yes.   We have statistics which show that the male sex has recourse to outlets on an average 4·8 times in a year, while the female sex has recourse to outlets only 1·9 times.

MABEL (*frigid*).   What do you mean by outlets ?

SHIRLEY.   Unfaithfulness.   " Outlets " is a technical term in our statistics office.

THERÈSE.   1·9 times ?   That means that every year you sleep with one man who is not your husband, and also with nine-tenths of another man ?

MABEL.   Really, what an extraordinary conversation.

THERÈSE.   I think it's all nonsense.   It proves nothing.

MABEL.   Hear, hear.

THERÈSE.   You can't dissociate a woman's behaviour from the man's.   The human element is completely lacking in all these figures, and a study of the human heart will tell you much more.

SHIRLEY.   I don't agree.   Well, if you're in the mood for experimenting, let's conduct a little poll here and now.

MABEL.   God forbid !

SHIRLEY.   Dr. Schultz says a healthy woman has nothing to hide.

MABEL.   I don't care what Doctor Schultz says.   Even if a woman has nothing to hide, she should be at great pains to hide it.

SHIRLEY.   Well, I'm modern !   I don't mind telling you girls that I need an outlet, perhaps even more than others, because I am emotionally attracted by psychological work—and then, my husband is an unusual and interesting mental specimen.

WESLEY. That's enough, Shirley !

WICKED FAIRY. She can't hear you.

SHIRLEY. He's got a strong streak of the infantile, the backward, in him, his mother's fault, of course.

WESLEY. Well, knock me down.

SHIRLEY. This side of Wesley's character does not satisfy the deeply mature side of my nature, and there you have clear evidence of maladjustment. Naturally, I have to find an element to satisfy my maturity elsewhere. An outlet, in fact. It's as simple as that.

MABEL. You might call it painfully simple.

SHIRLEY. Why ? Eradicate shame ! Why be inhibited ? Live, live, live.

MABEL (shocked). I do very well in my own way, thank you.

SHIRLEY. Yeah, I bet. Listen, I've had three outlets this year.

WESLEY (shouting). What ?

AIMÉ (to WESLEY). How many have you had, Wesley ?

WESLEY. Two, damn it.

SHIRLEY. I'm not ashamed. I wouldn't mind telling Wesley, he'd be interested to hear.

WESLEY. That's a lie !

SHIRLEY. He and I are friends.

WESLEY. That's a heresy !

SHIRLEY. But there, I've talked too much.

WESLEY. That's the first true thing you've said !

SHIRLEY. How about you, Mrs. Frappot ? After all, we're all girls together.

THERÈSE. Well . . . my husband is a typical man. Very kind ; very thoughtful—except when he is in love with someone else ; very cultivated ; very intelligent ; very handsome ; a very nice man ; not a wonderful husband.

AIMÉ. Her generosity is atrocious.

THERÈSE. He appreciates beauty perhaps too much, because he can never resist investigating it. He also adores intelligence, and an intelligent but ugly woman can make me more unhappy than a pretty face. To make matters more difficult, I like and admire his taste in these things. It is to me a little indiscriminate, but always discriminating. He always likes women, categorizes them, and if he flirts with them he knows exactly what he is doing, and can almost tell to a day how long an affair is going to last.   I love him very much.

SHIRLEY.   I see.   A high intelligence quotient.   And how do you respond ?   Passively ?

THERÈSE (*after a second's reflection*).   I have an agreement with a business man—a transport chief.

AIMÉ.   Ah, if that were only true !

SHIRLEY.   A steady date ?

THERÈSE.   Oh yes, for years.

SHIRLEY.   And no divorce ?

THERÈSE.   I'm in love with my husband . . .

AIMÉ (*pained*).   Oh . . .

SHIRLEY.   I see.   That brings our average to two.   Now, Mrs. Sparrow.

MABEL.   I refuse to discuss the matter.   I consider it absolutely scandalous.

SHIRLEY (*to* THERÈSE).   There's a great deal of tact involved in my work.   (*To* MABEL.)   Won't you even tell us about your husband ?

MABEL.   He's a rattling good sort.   There.   Are you satisfied ?

SHIRLEY.   That is hardly data, Mrs. Sparrow.

MABEL.   It was never intended to be.

SHIRLEY.   Is he virile and demanding ?

MABEL.   I'm sure I don't know what you mean.   He plays cricket.

SHIRLEY.   Athletic, huh ?

MABEL.   If you must know, extremely.   (*Bitterly.*)   Excessively.   Whenever I want to talk to him, he's either shadow-boxing or skipping.

DESMOND.   Oh, I say.

SHIRLEY.   I see.   Is he therefore intellectually a little dry, a little restricted ?

MABEL.   He's intellectually non-existent.   But then, I like that.   I loathe intellectuals of any shade or colour.   In my opinion, they are responsible for half the world's present misery.

DESMOND.   Oh dear, she's off.

MABEL.   D'you think we would have acquired our Empire if we had kept asking the whys and wherefores of things ?   And d'you think my husband would be the first-class administrator he is if he bothered to find out what other people thought ?   And could I run my Guide Company so that it wins an honourable mention in every jamboree if I spent half the time on thinking that I do on doing ? Certainly not.

SHIRLEY. So there is no intellectual starvation.

MABEL. I really don't know what you're talking about. Desmond is a regular officer. He's a bit of an amateur engineer, and he loves wild animals. And that's that.

SHIRLEY. Has he any other interests ? Does he write or draw ?

MABEL (*more deeply shocked than ever*). Certainly not !

SHIRLEY. And about him and women ?

MABEL. You are being quite unnecessarily disgusting, Mrs. Whateveritis.

SHIRLEY. And on the point of your infidelity, Mrs. Sparrow ?

MABEL (*terrible*). I am his wife !

SHIRLEY. I know that, but——

MABEL. That is quite enough of that !

WESLEY (*bitter*). Congratulations, old boy.

DESMOND (*sighing*). It isn't strictly true, you know. She gets drunk occasionally. At the Regimental dinner before last, she chased the Divisional Commander all over the Barracks . . .

SHIRLEY (*who has been doing a sum on an envelope*). The average is now 1·3. Now, Mrs. Ikonenko.

(*No reply.*)

IKONENKO. She doesn't speak English.

SHIRLEY. Madame, voulez-vous . . .

(*No reply.*)

DESMOND. Your wife doesn't say much, Ikonenko.

IKONENKO. She doesn't speak French either.

SHIRLEY. Frau Ikonenko, Wollen Sie bitte . . .

IKONENKO. She doesn't even speak much Russian. In fact, she hardly speaks at all.

WESLEY. What a godsend !

(*At that moment,* MME. IKONENKO *decides it's time to feed the child. With her back to the audience, she bares her breast, and places the child to it, humming an ancient lullaby.* MABEL *gazes at her, horrified.* THERÈSE *is whimsically amused, but* SHIRLEY *is visibly taken aback.*)

MABEL.   Well, really, what a place to choose.

SHIRLEY.   So insanitary !

THERÈSE.   You really mean, so public, so uncomplicated !

IKONENKO.   There ! Olga has done the first decent and feminine thing, and all the others are shocked.

AIMÉ.   Not Therèse ! Oh, Therèse, if only I loved you !

SHIRLEY (*a little confused*).   Well, anyway, there's evidence of an outlet there. That makes the average 1·25. Only ·65 of an error. You see, there is truth in figures.

(The MAYOR *enters.)*

MAYOR.   Good evening. Good evening, ladies. No sign of the Colonels yet ?

DESMOND.   Oh, not this cove again !

WICKED FAIRY (*smiling*).   Had enough ?

CHORUS.   Yes !

WICKED FAIRY.   Curtain !

(The curtain swings down.)

Well, what is your decision ?

WESLEY (*rising, livid*).   I'm going to get a divorce, that's what I'm going to do.

AIMÉ.   Why ?

WESLEY.   What d'you mean, why ? Didn't you see ?

AIMÉ.   I saw, and I suffered, for myself and for us all.

DESMOND.   Jolly decent of you.

AIMÉ.   But remember, we only see them as we saw ourselves before we came here. Reverse the situation. What would they have thought if they had eavesdropped on one of our conversations ? We don't know our wives. They don't know us. We are all alone, impenetrable jungles. How can we be happy ?

GOOD FAIRY.   Listen to me !

AIMÉ.   No ! You represent perfection. You don't know the difficulties of choice.

WICKED FAIRY (*bitter*).   Difficulties ? It's what we envy most in you.

AIMÉ.   But how do we know what is right and wrong ?

GOOD FAIRY.   I am right.

WICKED FAIRY (*slighted*).   So am I !

AIMÉ.   Ah, but when it is all mixed, in that jungle ! You are on rails, my friends—we have to walk a slippery road. We can't do right without not doing wrong, and we can't do wrong without not doing right. Every act is a renunciation of another. We must do one thing or the other, and when we do one thing, the other is undone.

DESMOND. I haven't your sort of architectural mind, Aimé.

AIMÉ. Donovan wants us to stay, because she knows the Beauty to be incorruptible. She wants us to reach for the unattainable in a vacuum. A cruel aim for such a pretty girl.

(*The* WICKED FAIRY *laughs*).

AIMÉ. Carabosse wanted us to rape perfection, to make his victory complete, to end his awful immortality.

WICKED FAIRY (*furious*). I can never forgive God for having invented the French.

AIMÉ. He has just now seen that it is hopeless. Now he wants us to return, so that we may lose ourselves again in the morass, open to temptation, wide-eyed and willing, the more so since we have just seen our wives.

DESMOND. I see. Well, whatever you may have to say, I'm going back.

(*The* WICKED FAIRY *laughs quietly.*)

There's one thing you've overlooked in my case, you see. I'm quite fond of Mabel, yes, but not in any special way, you understand—that was over a long time ago, just before I married her, to be precise. But I do badly want to see my dogs again—Ranger, Thunderbolt, and Black Havoc. And then . . . (*He laughs, shyly.*) . . . the Editor of *Field* said he was interested in a poem for the Christmas issue . . .

GOOD FAIRY (*sad*). So you're going back . . .

DESMOND. Yes. Sorry to let you down, Donovan, after all you've done. I'd have made you a Lance-Corporal if you weren't above all that.

IKONENKO. I too will return.

(*The* WICKED FAIRY *cackles.*)

GOOD FAIRY (*indignant*). Why ?

IKONENKO. Colonel Sparrow——

DESMOND. Rinder-Sparrow.

IKONENKO. Colonel Desmond is right when he says that his

love for his wife was over just before he married her. If we stayed, what would happen ? We would awake in a hundred years, and try to seduce the Beauty again, and again we would fail. Then we would return to life. My friends . . . Comrades . . . You have seen my wife. I can't boast about her, but I can't complain. I leave ideals to fools, and return to my duties as a Soviet officer with relief. I am not interested in horizons, gentlemen, I am interested in breathing, and I wish to forget this as quickly as possible, and return to the life I know, with all its inequalities and suffering and welcome constriction.

WICKED FAIRY. Excellent !

AIMÉ. Yes, a surprisingly intelligent assessment, if I may say so, but I am staying.

WICKED FAIRY (*aghast*). What ? You were the one I thought I could count on most !

GOOD FAIRY (*entranced*). Oh, Aimé !

AIMÉ. Listen. I have lived my life as an explorer in the world of women. It has been easy, fascinating, and often very beautiful, but it was all accessible, and therefore transitory. All that I have not experienced is the quest for the unattainable. I happened to marry Therèse. I could as easily have married any of the others. If I had married one of the others, I should probably have loved Therèse more. My dear fairies, you envy me my power to choose, but I am sick of choosing, for at the moment of choice, I always regret what I have not done. Therefore I long to give myself to the selfless and patient pursuit of a single elusive woman, whom, as a punishment, I shall never possess.

WESLEY. I guess I'm staying, too, though not from any clear motive. My whole life seems to me so incoherent and horrible that I just don't really know how to explain why I don't want to go back. There must have been a time I thought Shirley brilliant —just brilliant. But after being here, and seeing what made the four of us tick, she just seemed so damned pretentious, and . . . I don't know the word . . . insensitive ? . . . Yeah, that's it . . . insensitive . . . to my problems and everyone else's . . . well, what it boils down to, fellows . . . I need a rest. That's all, folks.

WICKED FAIRY. Two to you, and two to me.

GOOD FAIRY. An equitable score.

WICKED FAIRY (*wan*). It's something we have in common. (*Brisk*). All right, we'll put you to sleep. We'll give you comfortable beds on the stage. Say your farewells, if you will.

DESMOND. Good-bye, Aimé. I think you're mad.

AIMÉ. I enjoy taking myself by surprise. *Bon voyage*, Desmond.

IKONENKO. Good-bye. (*He salutes.*)

WESLEY. It's been fun, and I want you to know it.

(*General good-byes.*)

WICKED FAIRY. Right. Now, Aimé and Wesley, will you go onto the stage ?

DESMOND. Any message to your wives ?

WICKED FAIRY. That is not permitted. We will have to arrange an accident.

WESLEY. An accident ?

WICKED FAIRY. Your disappearance will have to be explained. The police are so much more active than they were even a hundred years ago. Donovan, come with me.

(*The* TWO FAIRIES *go into the wings.*)

DESMOND. Good-bye again, Wesley, old son.

WESLEY. Pitch right in there, Des. Yahoo !

(WESLEY *and* AIMÉ *disappear behind the curtain.*)

DESMOND. Extraordinary. Wesley's like a fellow with a great load off his mind. I say, you don't think we're being fools leaving them ?

IKONENKO. No.

DESMOND. And we're not in any sense letting them down, I suppose. I'd hate to do that.

IKONENKO. We are right and they are wrong.

DESMOND. I hope so.

IKONENKO. I too . . .

(IKONENKO *and* DESMOND *go off into the wings, but stop and turn back as the* WICKED FAIRY *and the* GOOD FAIRY *return from the other side of the stage, dressed as a Doctor and a Nurse.*)

WICKED FAIRY. Ideal clothes, you see. We'll arrive at the Control Commission Office as a Doctor and Nurse straight from the scene of the accident. You'll have to put on grave faces though.

IKONENKO. Mine is always grave.

[The curtains part. The decor is the first pastoral setting with two more beds, one on each side of BEAUTY. AIMÉ *and* WESLEY *are lying on them. The* WICKED FAIRY *and the* GOOD FAIRY *go onto the stage.)*

GOOD FAIRY. Aimé . . . Wesley . . . sleep . . . a dreamless sleep . . . Orchestra—sleep in five minutes—but until then, play !

(Soft music begins, the music of the beginning.)

WICKED FAIRY. Come on, no time to lose, back to the cold winds of the living world . . . into the air . . . away . . . away . . .

(The TWO FAIRIES, IKONENKO *and* DESMOND *sweep out. The* WICKED FAIRY'S *voice gets softer quickly.)*

AIMÉ *(quiet)*. Wesley, are you asleep ?
WESLEY. Not yet, brother . . .

(Pause. Their two hands reach out, and almost touch the BEAUTY.)*

Aimé . . . I can't reach the Beauty . . . can you ?
AIMÉ. No, not quite . . . it was arranged like this on purpose . . .

(Slight pause.)

WESLEY. Aimé ?
AIMÉ. Mm ?
WESLEY. Were we wrong not to go back ?
AIMÉ. What is the use of asking such a question ? At this precise moment, they are asking themselves if they were wrong not to stay . . .

CURTAIN.

LONDON
27th November, 1950